STREET TALK · 3
THE BEST OF
AMERICAN IDIOMS

To order the accompanying cassette for

STREET TALK·3

See the coupon on the last page for details

STREET TALK · 3
THE BEST OF
AMERICAN IDIOMS

David Burke

Publisher: Optima Books
Editor: Robert Graul
Managing Editor: Debbie Wright
Editing, Design, and Production: Optima PrePress
Front Cover Illustration: Ty Semaka
Inside Illustrations: Ty Semaka

Library of Congress Preassigned Catalog Card Number: 93-84787
ISBN 1-879440-12-1
Printed in the United States of America
95 10 9 8 7 6 5 4 3 2

This book is dedicated to my best friend Kim Isbister - a woman who is truly brilliant, charming, classy, hilarious, gifted, and beautiful... or so she tells me.

Preface

To the outsider, idioms seem like a confusing "secret" code reserved only for the native speaker of English. Idioms are certainly tricky beasts because it is the *sum* of all the words in the phrase which must be interpreted, not each word by itself. In other words, the listener must never confuse the literal translation of an idiom with the underlying meaning of what is really being expressed or symbolized. If you are told *"Get me a pizza... and step on it!"* you are not being instructed to go trample on a round piece of cheesy bread. You are simply being told to hurry, since *"step on it"* refers to "pressing down on" the accelerator of a car.

In addition, a common idiom such as *"to bend over backwards"* has nothing to do with acrobatics or flexibility. It's simply a colorful way of conveying that someone has to exert a great deal of effort in order to do something.

> *example:* I **bent over backwards** trying to help Richard.

> *translation:* I exerted a great deal of effort trying to help Richard.

In short, idioms are simply an imaginative and expressive way to communicate an idea or thought. In order to be considered proficient in English, idioms must be learned since they are consistently used in books, magazines, television, movies, songs, American homes, etc.

For the non-native speaker, learning the information in **STREET TALK -3** will equal years of living in America and reduce the usual time it takes to absorb the intricacies of slang and colloquialisms.

For the American, you're in for a treat as we explore the evolution and variations of some of the most common and hilarious idiomatic expressions that have been with us, and will stay with us through the years.

STREET TALK -3 is a self-teaching guide made up of fourteen chapters, each divided into four primary parts:

- **DIALOGUE**

  Ten popular American idioms (indicated in boldface) are presented as they may be heard in an actual conversation. A translation of the dialogue in standard English is always given on the opposite page followed by an important phonetic version of the dialogue as it would actually be spoken by an American. This page will prove vital to any non-native since Americans tend to rely heavily on contractions, reductions, and other shortcuts in pronunciation.

- **VOCABULARY**

  This section spotlights all of the idioms that were used in the dialogue and offers two examples of usage for each entry, including synonyms, antonyms, and special notes.

- **PRACTICE THE VOCABULARY**

  These word games include all of the idioms previously learned and will help you to test yourself on your comprehension. (The pages providing the answers to all the drills are indicated at the beginning of this section.)

- **DICTATION (Test your oral comprehension)**

  Using an optional audio cassette *(see coupon on back page),* the student will hear a paragraph containing many of the idioms from opening dialogue. The paragraph will be read *as it would actually be heard* in a conversation, using frequent contractions and reductions.

NOTE: Some chapters offer a special section where the reader will be given an up close look at common idioms pertaining to a specific category such as alliterations, repeating words, proverbs, and survival idioms.

At the end of each five chapters is a review exam encompassing all of the words and expressions learned up to that point.

If you have always prided yourself on being fluent in English, you will undoubtedly be surprised and amused to encounter a whole new world of phrases usually hidden away in the American-English language and usually reserved only for the native speaker...*until now!*

David Burke
Author

NOTE

STREET TALK -1: How to Speak & Understand American Slang focuses on common slang and idioms used in everyday life. In addition, this first volume provides the reader with a thorough understanding of the frequent contractions, reductions and shortcuts in speech used by virtually every native speaker of English.

STREET TALK -2: Slang Used in Popular American Television Shows spotlights some of the most popular slang terms used in American television. Topics include slang and idioms used in today's television comedies, dramas, news reports, sports, traffic reports, commercials, weather reports, general entertainment, etc.

Acknowledgments

An emormous, gargantuan, humongous, *"Mondo-thank you!"* goes to Jody Stern for her suggestion and motivation to write a book solely on American idioms. Her insight, enthusiasm, and creativity are, as always, highly valued.

I am very thankful to Ty Semaka, our illustrator and cover artist. His creativity, professionalism, and ability to produce exceptional images were astounding.

Once again, a special thanks goes to Janet Graul, Vivian Margolin, and Debbie Wright for making the copy-editing phase of this book so enjoyable. Their patience, expertise, and attitude are so appreciated.

I owe a special debt of gratitude to all of the people throughout the U.S. that I hounded for information regarding slang, idioms, and gestures. I was always met with kindness and an eagerness to offer a total stranger some, oftentimes bizarre, information.

And of course, *"Thanks Ma!"*

Legend

boldface words in parentheses are used before the main entry – they appear after the main entry for alphabetization purposes only:
i.e. *the blind leading the blind*

expression

blind leading the blind (the) *exp.* said of a situation where an inexperienced person is being taught by someone equally inexperienced.

usage example:

You're teaching Ann to drive? Talk about **the blind leading the blind**!

translation:

You're teaching Ann to drive? This is an example of an inexperienced person teaching another inexperienced person!

NOTE: *"Talk about..."* is an extremely popular expression meaning "This is certainly an example of..."

useful information about the preceding entry

noun

literal translation

cop *n.* police officer.

go without a snag (to) *exp.* said of a project or event that proceeds smoothly • "snag" (lit); a break or tear in fabric].

bracketed words in the main entry are optional

hit the nail [right] on the head (to) *exp.* to be exactly right.

an equivalent term or expression of the main entry in boldface

SYNONYM: **to be dead on** *exp.*

a term or expression opposite in meaning of the main entry in boldface

ANTONYM: **to be way off base** *exp.* to be absolutely incorrect.

shut up (to) *v.* to stop talking.

spitting image of someone (to be the) *exp.* to be identical to someone.

verb

VARIATION: **to be the spit and image of someone** *exp.* • *He's the spit and image of his father; He looks just like his father.*

a common variation of the main entry in boldface

x

Table of Contents

Chapters 1-10
Popular Idioms

Chapters 11-14
Specialty Idioms

Bernie was always hoping for a **"fair shake."**

Lesson One - POPULAR IDIOMS

I'm sure they'll "give you a fair shake"

DIALOGUE

Debbie and Valerie are at an audition for the school musical.

Debbie: I can't believe I let you **talk me into** auditioning for the school musical. When I get this nervous, I can't **carry a tune**. Look at me! I'm **breaking out in a cold sweat**!

Valerie: Would you please stop **going off the deep end** and try **to get a hold of yourself**?

Debbie: You're right. I'm **blowing this all out of proportion**. It's just that every time I audition for anything, I feel like I've been **put through a wringer** when it's all over. I just want them **to give me a fair shake**. That's all I ask.

Valerie: Hey, there's Nancy. She's the best singer in the entire school. I didn't know she was going to audition for the same part as you.

Debbie: **That does it**! I'm leaving. I **don't have a prayer**.

2

Lesson One - POPULAR IDIOMS

Translation of dialogue in standard English

DIALOGUE

Debbie and Valerie are at an audition for the school musical.

Debbie: I can't believe I let you **convince me to** audition for the school musical. When I get this nervous, I can't **sing a melody on pitch**. Look at me! I'm **starting to sweat from fear!**

Valerie: Would you please stop **panicking** and try **to get control of yourself**?

Debbie: You're right. I'm **starting to think that this is more important than it really is**. It's just that every time I audition for anything, I feel **totally exhausted** when it's all over. I just want them **to give me a fair chance**. That's all I ask.

Valerie: Hey, there's Nancy. She's the best singer in the entire school. I didn't know she was going to audition for the same part as you.

Debbie: **That's all I can tolerate!** I'm leaving. I don't have **any chance of succeeding**.

Dialogue in slang as it would be heard

I'm sher they'll "give you a fair shake"

DIALOGUE

Debbie 'n Valerie 'r ad 'n audition fer the school musical.

Debbie: I can't b'lieve I let chew **talk me inta** auditioning fer the school musical. When I get this nervous, I can't **carry a tune**. Look 'it me! I'm **breaking oud 'n a cold sweat**!

Valerie: Would ju please stop **goin' off the deep end** 'n try **ta ged a hold 'a yerself**?

Debbie: Y'r right. I'm **blowin' this all oudda proportion**. It's jus' thad ev'ry time I audition fer anything, I feel like I've been **put through a wringer** when it's all over. I jus' want 'em **ta gimme a fair shake**. That's all I ask.

Valerie: Hey, there's Nancy. She's the bes' singer 'n the entire school. I did'n' know she was gonna audition fer the same pard as you.

Debbie: **That does it**! I'm leaving. I **don' have a prayer**.

AUTHOR NOTE

The reductions encountered above (as well as throughout the rest of this book) are used by virtually every native-born American. It is also common among many people to reduce the *-ing* ending to *-in'* such as *fishin', golfin', walkin', etc. (I'm goin' fishin' today)*. However, it is important to note that the reduction of *-ing* is considered to be somewhat unrefined.

4

Vocabulary

blow something [all] out of proportion (to) *exp.* to exaggerate.

usage example (1):   Mike's airplane trip was a little bumpy but he's been telling everyone the airplane almost crashed! He sure does **blow everything [all] out of proportion**.

translation: Mike's airplane trip was a little bumpy but he's been telling everyone the airplane almost crashed! He sure does exaggerate.

usage example (2):   Sam and Julie had a little disagreement. The way you told me about it, I thought they were going to get divorced! You sure have a tendency **to blow things [all] out of proportion**!

translation: Sam and Julie had a little disagreement. The way you told me about it, I thought they were going to get divorced! You sure have a tendency to exaggerate!

SYNONYM: **to make something into a bigger deal than it is** *exp.*

usage example: Why are you getting so upset just because I'm two minutes late? You're **making this into a bigger deal than it is**.

translation: Why are you getting so upset just because I'm two minutes late? You're exaggerating this entire situation.

break out in a cold sweat (to) *exp.* to begin perspiring suddenly due to great fear or anxiety.

usage example (1):   When I heard about the earthquake near my parents' house, I **broke out in a cold sweat**.

translation: When I heard about the earthquake near my parents' house, I began perspiring suddenly (due to anxiety).

usage example (2): I **broke out in a cold sweat** when I saw the tornado coming closer.

translation: I began perspiring suddenly from fear when I saw the tornado coming closer.

NOTE: The expression *"to break out"* means "to develop (a physical condition)."

usage example: I just **broke out** in a rash.

translation: I just developed a rash.

carry a tune (to) *exp.* said of someone who is able to sing on pitch.

usage example (1): I'm not really a singer but at least I can **carry a tune**.

translation: I'm not really a singer but at least I can sing on pitch.

usage example (2): You want Peter to join our choir? He can't **carry a tune**!

translation: You want Peter to join our choir? He can't sing on pitch!

fair shake (to give someone a) *exp.* to give someone the same fair treatment as you would give to others.

usage example (1): Do you think the jury will give the defendant a **fair shake**?

translation: Do you think the jury will give the defendant a fair trial?

usage example (2): At the choir audition, I was only allowed to sing one verse but Natalie was allowed to sing her entire song! I don't think I got a **fair shake**.

translation: At the choir audition, I was only allowed to sing one verse but Natalie was allowed to sing her entire song! I don't think I was treated fairly.

get a hold of oneself (to) *exp.* to get control of one's emotions.

usage example (1): **Get a hold of yourself**! I've never seen you so upset before!

translation: Get control of your emotions! I've never seen you so upset before!

usage example (2): I'm not going to let her drive anywhere until she **gets a hold of herself**. I don't think she can drive safely in her current emotional state.

translation: I'm not going to let her drive anywhere until she gets control of her emotions. I don't think she can drive safely in her current emotional state.

SYNONYM (1): **to get a grip** *exp.*

usage example: **Get a grip**!

translation: Get control of yourself!

SYNONYM (2): **to pull oneself together** *exp.*

usage example: You've got **to pull yourself together**!

translation: You've got to get control of your emotions!

go off the deep end (to) *exp.* • 1. to become upset and irrational • 2. to become crazy.

usage example (1): My teacher **went off the deep end** because I was late to class again.

translation: My teacher got really upset because I was late to class again.

usage example (2): After Mr. Fletcher's wife died, he **went off the deep end**.

translation: After Mr. Fletcher's wife died, he went crazy.

SYNONYM: **to flip out** *exp.*

usage example (1): Sandra **flipped out** when she saw her boyfriend with another woman.

translation: Sandra became extremely upset when she saw her boyfriend with another woman.

usage example (2): Bernie was always a well respected man. It was such a surprise when he **flipped out** and committed murder!

translation: Bernie was always a well respected man. It was such a surprise when he went crazy and committed murder!

I think Earl has finally gone **"off the deep end."**

prayer (not to have a) *exp.* to have no possibility of success in something.

usage example (1): You **don't have a prayer** of beating Andy at chess.

translation: You don't have any possibility of beating Andy at chess.

usage example (2): I **don't have a prayer** of passing my geometry test tomorrow. I should have studied harder.

translation: I don't have a possible chance of passing my geometry test tomorrow. I should have studied harder.

ANTONYM: **to have a [good] shot at something** *exp.* to have a [good] possibility at success in something.

usage example: Don't you think Dan **has a shot** at getting the job?

translation: Don't you think Dan has a chance of getting the job?

talk someone into something (to) *exp.* to convince someone to do something.

usage example (1): Michelle said she didn't want to go with us to the movies. Why don't you try and **talk her into it**? I just know she'd have a good time.

translation: Michelle said she didn't want to go with us to the movies. Why don't you try to convince her? I just know she'd have a good time.

usage example (2):   You **talked me into it**. I'll give you one more chance to take the test.

translation: You convinced me. I'll give you one more chance to take the test.

ANTONYM: **to talk someone out of something** *exp.* to convince someone not to do something.

usage example: I was going to accept the job position of manager, but Earl **talked me out of it**. He said it would be too much work and long hours.

translation: I was going to accept the job position of manager, but Earl convinced me not to accept it. He said it would be too much work and long hours.

"That does it!" *exp.* "That's all I can tolerate!"

usage example (1):   **That does it**! If you ever borrow anything from me again without asking, you're in big trouble!

translation: That's all I can tolerate! If you ever borrow anything from me again without asking, you're in big trouble!

usage example (2):   My bicycle just broke again! **That does it**! I'm buying a new one tomorrow.

translation: My bicycle just broke again! That's all I can tolerate! I'm buying a new one tomorrow.

SYNONYM: **"That tears it!"** *exp.*

usage example: **That tears it**! If the boss doesn't give me a raise, I'm quitting!

translation: That's all I can tolerate! If the boss doesn't give me a raise, I'm quitting!

through a/the wringer (to put someone) *exp.* to put someone through a strenuous and emotional experience.

usage example (1):　Why didn't you call to tell me you were going to be three hours late coming home? I was so worried. You really **put me through a wringer**!

translation:　Why didn't you call to tell me you were going to be three hours late coming home? I was so worried. You really caused me a great deal of emotional turmoil!

usage example (2):　I was really **put through the wringer** at my job interview. I had to fill out papers, meet dozens of people, and do a presentation!

translation:　I was really put through a strenuous experience at my job interview. I had to fill out papers, meet dozens of people, and do a presentation!

NOTE:　In the early days of washing machines, it was common to put the laundry through a device known as a *"wringer"* before hanging the clothing outside to dry. This device was comprised of two rollers between which the clothing was pressed, squeezing out any excess water. The above expression, depicts someone who is emotionally drained or *"squeezed"* dry.

Practice The Vocabulary

(Answers to Lesson 1, p. 258)

A. Choose the correct phrase that best completes the sentence or thought.

1. **You talked me into it...**
   - ☐ a. I don't want you to borrow my car.
   - ☐ b. I'll let you borrow my car.
   - ☐ c. You confused me.

2. **Helen went off the deep end when...**
   - ☐ a. she won the car.
   - ☐ b. her boss gave her a raise.
   - ☐ c. she got fired.

3. **I didn't get a fair shake at the job interview...**
   - ☐ a. I was only interviewed for two minutes.
   - ☐ b. The interviewer spent a lot of time with me.
   - ☐ c. I got hired right after the interview.

4. **Bill can't carry a tune...**
   - ☐ a. Let's ask him to sing at our wedding.
   - ☐ b. Let's find someone else to sing at our wedding.
   - ☐ c. He sings beautifully.

5. **I broke out in a cold sweat when...**
   - ☐ a. I won the contest.
   - ☐ b. I heard the good news.
   - ☐ c. I heard the front door open in the middle of the night.

6. **You don't have a prayer of winning the lottery...**
   - ☐ a. Spend your money on something else.
   - ☐ b. Buy a ticket for me, too!
   - ☐ c. I think you're going to win!

7. **That does it!...**
   - ☐ a. He gave me such a nice compliment.
   - ☐ b. He insulted me for the last time!
   - ☐ c. I'm so glad I came to this party.

8. **I feel like I've been put through a wringer...**
   - ☐ a. It was so much fun!
   - ☐ b. What a great day!
   - ☐ c. What a horrible day!

B. CONTEXT EXERCISE
Choose the idiom from the right column that goes with the phrase in the left column.

☐ 1. You're going to ask Kim out on a date?

A. You're really **blowing this [all] out of proportion**.

☐ 2. When Bob went to apply for a new job, he was only given a two-minute interview.

B. I've never seen anyone **go off the deep end** like that before.

☐ 3. You want Janet to join our choir?

C. Okay. You **talked me into it**. I'll see you tonight.

☐ 4. I know you want me to reconsider and join you for diner, but I have homework to do.

D. **That does it**! I'm firing him right now.

☐ 5. I had a very hard day.

E. I don't think he was **given a fair shake**.

☐ 6. When Susan's cat died, she cried for days and stopped eating.

F. I feel like I've been **put through a wringer**.

☐ 7. I can't believe how angry you are that I forgot to close the garage door!

G. She can't even **carry a tune**!

☐ 8. Is he making personal phone calls on the job again?

H. You **don't have a prayer**. I don't think she even likes you.

C. CROSSWORD
Fill in the crossword puzzle on the opposite page by choosing the correct word(s) from the list below.

blowing
cold sweat
deep
fair shake
get a hold

prayer
talk me into
that does it
tune
wringer

Across

12. My sister is a great singer, but I can't even carry a _____ .

19. I don't have a _____ of being promoted. The other candidate for the promotion is the owner's nephew.

26. You don't have to _____ doing you a favor. I'd be happy to help you!

36. Why are you getting so angry? It was an accident. I don't know why you're _____ this thing all out of proportion!

Down

2. I broke out in a _____ when my car broke down in the worst part of the city.

4. You're going to interview Mike for a job? You don't even like him. How can you possibly give him a _____ ?

7. Craig went off the _____ end when Joe dented his car. I've never seen anyone get so angry!

12. _____ ! I'm not going to tolerate this anymore!

17. I've never been so worried in my life. I feel like I've been put through a _____ .

24. I've never seen you so upset before. You've got to _____ of yourself and examine this problem calmly.

CROSSWORD PUZZLE

D. Complete the dialogue using the appropriate idioms from the list below.

[all] out of proportion	prayer
fair shake	put through a wringer
get a hold of yourself	talk me into
go off the deep end	that does it

Peter: I've never seen you this angry before! You've got to

(1)_____ . You've been

screaming at everyone all day. It's not like you to

(2)_____ like this.

Greg: I know you must think I'm blowing everything

(3)_____ but I wasn't

given a **(4)**_____ at my job interview today.

I never should have let you **(5)**_____ going.

Peter: **(6)**_____! I'm tired of being blamed for

everything that happens to you!

Greg: I'm sorry. It's just that I feel like I've been **(7)**_____

_____. I guess I knew I

didn't have a **(8)**_____ of getting

the job anyway.

E. DICTATION
Test Your Oral Comprehension
(This dictation can be found in Appendix A on page 275).

If you are following along with your cassette, you will now hear a paragraph containing many of the idioms from this section. The paragraph will be read by a native speaker at normal conversational speed (which may seem fast to you at first). In addition, the words will be pronounced *as you would actually hear them in a conversation,* including many common reductions.

The first time the paragraph is presented, simply listen in order to get accustomed to the speed and heavy use of reductions. The paragraph will then be read again with a pause after each group of words to give you time to write down what you heard. The third time the paragraph is read, follow along with what you have written.

Lesson Two - POPULAR IDIOMS

"It's as plain as the nose on your face!"

Dialogue In Slang

"It's as plain as the nose on your face!"

DIALOGUE

Dave and Brad are standing outside the library when they notice Joe.

Dave: Hey, there's Joe. I wonder why he's **walking arm in arm** with that young woman.

Brad: It's **as plain as the nose on your face**. They're **going together**.

Dave: You're **pulling my leg**! She must be twenty years younger than Joe. Talk about **robbing the cradle**!

Brad: Well, you can bet this relationship's going to be a **flash in the pan**.

Dave: It must have been **love at first sight** because I know he didn't have a girlfriend last week.

Brad: I think you **hit the nail on the head**. Actually, my father **popped the question** to my mother after knowing her only two weeks. They **tied the knot** a month later!

Lesson Two - POPULAR IDIOMS

Translation In Standard English

DIALOGUE

Dave and Brad are standing outside the library when they notice Joe.

Dave: Hey, there's Joe. I wonder why he's **walking with his arm interlocked** in that young woman's arm.

Brad: It's **very obvious**. They're **dating each other**.

Dave: You're **kidding**! She must be twenty years younger than Joe. Talk about **dating someone much younger than you**!

Brad: Well, you can bet this relationship's **going to be temporary**.

Dave: It must have been **a case of falling in love at the first encounter** because I know he didn't have a girlfriend last week.

Brad: I think you're **absolutely right**. Actually, my father **proposed to my mother** after knowing her only two weeks. They **got married** a month later!

Lesson Two - POPULAR IDIOMS

Dialogue in slang as it would be heard

"It's ez plain ez the nose on yer face!"

DIALOGUE

Dave 'n Brad 'r standing outside the library when they nodice Joe.

Dave: Hey, there's Joe. I wonder why 'e'z **walking arm 'n arm** with that young woman.

Brad: It's **ez plain ez the nose on yer face**. They're **going together**.

Dave: Y'r **pulling my leg**! She mus' be twen'y years younger th'n Joe. Talk about **robbing the cradle**!

Brad: Well, you c'n bet this relationship's gonna be a **flash 'n the pan**.

Dave: It must've been **love 'it firs' sight** b'cause I know 'e didn't have a girlfriend last week.

Brad: I think ya **hit the nail on the head**. Akshelly, my father **popped the question** ta my mother after knowing 'er only two weeks. They **tied the knod** a month lader!

20

Vocabulary

as plain as the nose on one's face (to be) *exp.* to be obvious.

usage example (1): I can't believe you have no idea who stole the money from your office. It's **as plain as the nose on your face**!

translation: I can't believe you have no idea who stole the money from your office. It's obvious!

usage example (2): How can you tell me you don't know why she's mad at you? It's **as plain as the nose on your face**. You forgot her birthday.

translation: How can you tell me you don't know why she's mad at you? It's obvious. You forgot her birthday.

flash in the pan (to be a) *exp.* to be quick and temporary.

usage example (1): His success was only a **flash in the pan**.

translation: His success was only quick and temporary.

usage example (2): Steve's acting career was a **flash in the pan**.

translation: Steve's acting career was quick and temporary.

go together (to) *exp.* to be dating on a steady basis (said of two people in a relationship).

usage example (1): Jan and Paul are getting married? I didn't even know they were **going together**!

translation: Jan and Paul are getting married? I didn't even know they were dating each other!

usage example (2): After **going together** for almost three years, Mark and Stephanie just ended their relationship.

translation: After dating each other for almost three years, Mark and Stephanie just ended their relationship.

hit the nail [right] on the head (to) *exp.* to be absolutely correct.

usage example (1):   "How did he get to be promoted to supervisor? His father must be the president of the company."
"I think you **hit the nail [right] on the head**!"

translation: "How did he get to be promoted to supervisor? His father must be the president of the company."
"I think you're absolutely correct!

usage example (2):   When you called him a liar, I think you **hit the nail on the head**.

translation: When you called him a liar, I think you were absolutely correct.

SYNONYM: **to be dead on** *exp.*

usage example: You were **dead on** when you said not to trust her. She stole hundreds of dollars from the company!

translation: You were absolutely correct when you said not to trust her. She stole hundreds of dollars from the company!

ANTONYM: **to be way off base** *exp.* to be absolutely incorrect.

usage example: If you think David's going to give you a present, you're **way off base**.

translation: If you think David's going to give you a present, you're absolutely wrong.

love at first sight (to be) *exp.* said of a situation where two people fall in love upon first glance.

usage example (1):   With my mom and dad, it was **love at first sight**.

translation: With my mom and dad, they fell in love as soon as they saw each other.

usage example (2):   I know I've only known Marsha for a day, but I think we're going to get married some day. It was **love at first sight** for both of us.

translation: I know I've only known Marsha for a day, but I think we're going to get married some day. We fell in love as soon as we saw each other.

"Love at first sight..."

pop the question (to) *exp.* to propose marriage.

usage example (1): I think Steve is finally going **to pop the question** tonight!

translation: I think Steve is finally going to propose tonight!

usage example (2): Allen walked right into my office and **popped the question**!

translation: Allen walked right into my office and asked me to marry him!

pull someone's leg (to) *exp.* to kid someone; to tease.

usage example (1): You just found five hundred dollars? Are you **pulling my leg**?

translation: You just found five hundred dollars? Are you kidding me?

usage example (2): Mitch got a promotion? You're **pulling my leg**.

translation: Mitch got a promotion? You're kidding me.

rob the cradle (to) *exp.* to date someone much younger than oneself, to be dating a "baby."

usage example (1): Karen's date is young enough to be her son. She certainly is **robbing the cradle**!

translation: Karen's date is young enough to be her son. She certainly is dating someone much younger!

usage example (2): Carol is much younger than you think. Believe me, you're **robbing the cradle**.

translation: Carol is much younger than you think. Believe me, you're dating someone who's much younger than you.

tie the knot (to) *exp.* to get married.

usage example (1): Nancy and Dominic are going **to tie the knot** next week.

translation: Nancy and Dominic are going to get married next week.

usage example (2): This is the third time Jack's **tied the knot.**

translation: This is the third time Jack's gotten married.

SYNONYM: **to get hitched** *exp.* • (lit); to tie together.

usage example: I'm **getting hitched** tomorrow!

translation: I'm getting married tomorrow!

walk arm in arm (to) *exp.* to walk with one's arm curled through someone else's arm; arms linked or intertwined.

usage example (1): I think they're best friends. They always **walk arm in arm** everywhere they go.

translation: I think they're best friends. They always walk with their arms linked.

usage example (2): In Europe, it's very common to see women **walking arm in arm**.

translation: In Europe, it's very common to see women walking with their arms intertwined.

NOTE: SEE: *A CLOSER LOOK: More Repeating Words, p. 198*

Practice The Vocabulary

(Answers to Lesson 2, p. 259)

A. Are the following idioms used correctly or incorrectly?

1. She wins every contest she enters. Her luck is a **flash in the pan**.
   ☐ correct usage   ☐ incorrect usage

2. You're wrong. You **hit the nail on the head**.
   ☐ correct usage   ☐ incorrect usage

3. Steve just **popped the question**! He asked me to marry him!
   ☐ correct usage   ☐ incorrect usage

4. Sarah and Bill **tied the knot** yesterday. Did you go to their wedding?
   ☐ correct usage   ☐ incorrect usage

5. I think Jim's **robbing the cradle**. He's dating someone twice his age.
   ☐ correct usage   ☐ incorrect usage

6. Did you know that Gordon and Jeannie are **going together**? Maybe they'll get married some day.
   ☐ correct usage   ☐ incorrect usage

7. The explanation isn't clear at all. It's **as plain as the nose on your face**.
   ☐ correct usage   ☐ incorrect usage

8. He's always **pulling my leg**. He never jokes.
   ☐ correct usage   ☐ incorrect usage

B. Choose the correct answer from the list below.

a flash in the pan   robbing the cradle
as plain as the nose on your face   to pop the question
going together   to tie the knot
hit the nail on the head   to walk arm in arm
love at first sight   you're pulling my leg

1. Something quick and temporary is called:

   Answer:_____

2. When two people are dating, they are:

   Answer:_____

3. What is an idiom for "to ask someone to get married?"

   Answer:_____

4. When two people fall in love after seeing each other for the first time, this is called:

   Answer:_____

5. A person who dates someone much younger is said to be:

   Answer:_____

6. If something is obvious, it is:

   Answer:_____

7. What is an idiom for "to get married?"

   Answer:_____

8. What is a good response to give someone who is teasing you?

   Answer:_____

9. When you guess something exactly, you have:

   Answer:_____

10. Another way of saying "to walk with an arm linked through another person's arm" is:

    Answer:_____

C. Underline the word that best completes the phrase.

1. That's right! You hit the nail on the (**head, foot, arm**).

2. You're dating someone so young! People are going to say you're (**stealing, robbing, taking**) the cradle.

3. You don't know what the solution is to the problem? It's as plain as the (**eye, mouth, nose**) on your face!

4. You're getting married? When did Greg (**explode, burst, pop**) the question?

5. Nancy had triplets? You're pulling my (**hair, arm, leg**)!

6. His career isn't going to last long. It's going to be nothing more than a flash in the (**pan, skillet, pot**).

7. They fell in love as soon as they saw each other. It was love at (**first, second, third**) sight.

8. I heard you're getting married. So, when are you going to (**lace, tie, fasten**) the knot?

D. Choose the definition of the idiom in boldface.

1. Are you **pulling my leg**? Mark was just voted class president?
   - ☐ a. trying to hurt me
   - ☐ b. kidding me
   - ☐ c. trying to get my attention

2. We're going **to tie the knot** next week.
   - ☐ a. to quit our job
   - ☐ b. to find a new job
   - ☐ c. to get married

3. I think you **hit the nail on the head**.
   - ☐ a. are absolutely correct
   - ☐ b. are absolutely wrong
   - ☐ c. are totally confused

4. It's **as plain as the nose on your face**!
   - ☐ a. obvious
   - ☐ b. not very obvious
   - ☐ c. a ridiculous situation

5. Did you see the girl he's dating? He's definitely **robbing the cradle**.
   - ☐ a. dating someone a lot younger than he is
   - ☐ b. dating someone a lot smarter than he is
   - ☐ c. dating someone a lot older than he is

6. Their relationship's going to be **a flash in the pan**.
   - ☐ a. long-lasting
   - ☐ b. temporary
   - ☐ c. exciting

7. We've been **going together** for three years.
   - ☐ a. married
   - ☐ b. fighting
   - ☐ c. dating each other

8. Did Steve finally **pop the question**?
   - ☐ a. ask an unexpected question
   - ☐ b. propose marriage
   - ☐ c. start dating someone much younger

E. DICTATION
Test Your Oral Comprehension
(This dictation can be found in Appendix A on page 276).

If you are following along with your cassette, you will now hear a paragraph containing many of the idioms from this section. The paragraph will be read by a native speaker at normal conversational speed (which may seem fast to you at first). In addition, the words will be pronounced *as you would actually hear them in a conversation,* including many common reductions.

The first time the paragraph is presented, simply listen in order to get accustomed to the speed and heavy use of reductions. The paragraph will then be read again with a pause after each group of words to give you time to write down what you heard. The third time the paragraph is read, follow along with what you have written.

I think John's **"getting cold feet!"**

Dialogue In Slang

I think John's "getting cold feet!"

DIALOGUE

John just wrecked his father's car.

Steve: You've got to **break the news** to your father about wrecking his car. He'll understand it wasn't your fault. Your father's got a **good head on his shoulders**. I'm sure he'll **let you off the hook**.

John: Are you kidding? He's going **to fly off the handle**. Do you know how much money he had **to fork over** for this car?

Steve: Well, you're going to have **to face the music** eventually.

John: You're right. I'm going right inside and **come clean** with him. **On second thought**, why don't you tell him for me? I've **got cold feet**.

Steve: Don't worry. **If worse comes to worst**, you can just work three jobs for the rest of your life to pay him back!

Lesson Three - POPULAR IDIOMS

Translation   In Standard English

DIALOGUE

John just wrecked his father's car.

Steve: You've got to **announce to your father delicately** about wrecking his car. He'll understand it wasn't your fault. Your father's **very rational**. I'm sure he **won't hold you responsible**.

John: Are you kidding? He's going **to be furious**. Do you know how much money he had **to spend** for this car?

Steve: Well, you're going to have **to confront the situation** eventually.

John: You're right. I'm going right inside and **be honest** with him. **Upon reconsideration**, why don't you tell him for me? I lost **courage**.

Steve: Don't worry. **In the worst possible case**, you can just work three jobs for the rest of your life to pay him back!

Dialogue in slang as it would be heard

I think John's "gedding cold feet!"

DIALOGUE

John just wrecked 'is father's car.

Steve: You gotta **break the news** ta yer father about wrecking 'is car. He'll understand it wasn' cher fault. Yer father's god a **good head on 'is shoulders**. I'm sher 'e'll **let chew off the hook**.

John: Are you kidding? He's gonna **fly off the handle**. Do you know how much money he had **ta fork over** fer this car?

Steve: Well, y'r gonna haf **ta face the music** avenchally.

John: Y'r right. I'm going ride inside 'n **come clean** with 'im. **On secon' thought**, why don' chew tell 'im for me? I've **got cold feet**.

Steve: Don't worry. **If wors' comes ta worst**, you c'n jus' work three jobs fer the rest'a yer life ta pay 'im back!

Vocabulary

break the news to someone (to) *exp.* to disclose sensitive and emotional information to someone.

> *usage example (1):*   The veterinarian just called and told me my brother's dog died. I don't know how I'm going **to break the news** to him.

> *translation:*   The veterinarian just called and told me my brother's dog died. I don't know how I'm going to disclose such emotional information to him.

> *usage example (2):*   I just ruined my father's favorite sweater. I guess I'd better go **break the news** to him before he finds out from someone else.

> *translation:*   I just ruined my father's favorite sweater. I guess I'd better go disclose that to him before he finds out from someone else.

cold feet (to get) *exp.* to lose courage.

> *usage example (1):*   I was going to ask my boss for a raise but as soon as I saw him, I got **cold feet**.

> *translation:*   I was going to ask my boss for a raise but as soon as I saw him, I lost courage.

> *usage example (2):*   I know you asked me to tell Matt he's fired, but I just couldn't. I got **cold feet**.

> *translation:*   I know you asked me to tell Matt he's fired, but I just couldn't. I lost courage.

come clean (to) *exp.* to be honest (and confess the truth).

> *usage example (1):*   **Come clean** with me. Did you borrow my car while I was out of town?

translation: Be honest with me. Did you borrow my car while I was out of town?

usage example (2): Did you **come clean** with the teacher about cheating on the test?

translation: Did you confess to the teacher about cheating on the test?

face the music (to) *exp.* to confront an uncomfortable situation.

usage example (1): Our house guest has stayed with us an extra two weeks and he's making us crazy. I've been avoiding asking him to leave but I think it's finally time **to face the music**.

translation: Our house guest has stayed with us an extra two weeks and he's making us crazy. I've been avoiding asking him to leave but I think it's finally time to confront the situation.

usage example (2): You really should tell your mother what you did. You're going to have **to face the music** eventually.

translation: You really should tell your mother what you did. You're going to have to confront the situation eventually.

fly off the handle (to) *exp.* to lose one's temper.

usage example (1): My father **flew off the handle** when the neighbor's dog started barking in the middle of the night.

translation: My father lost his temper when the neighbor's dog started barking in the middle of the night.

usage example (2): Susan **flew off the handle** because I was five minutes late.

translation: Susan lost her temper because I was five minutes late.

Manny "flew off the handle" trying to learn a new computer program.

fork over (to) *exp.* to pay for something.

> *usage example (1):* How much money did you have **to fork over** for that new car?

> *translation:* How much money did you have to pay for that new car?

> *usage example (2):* I had **to fork over** two hundred dollars to buy this dress.

> *translation:* I had to pay two hundred dollars to buy this dress.

> **ALSO:** **to fork over** *exp.* to give.

> > *usage example:* That's mine! **Fork it over**!

> > *translation:* That's mine! Give it to me!

have a good head on one's shoulders (to) *exp.* said of
someone who is very intelligent and rational.

usage example (1): Tom **has a good head on his shoulders**. I'm sure he'll make the right decision about which house to buy.

translation: Tom is very intelligent and rational. I'm sure he'll make the right decision about which house to buy.

usage example (2): I'm promoting you to the position of manager. I've been looking for someone with a **good head on his shoulders** for a long time.

translation: I'm promoting you to the position of manager. I've been looking for someone who is very intelligent and rational for a long time.

"If worse comes to worst..." *exp.* "In the worst possible case..."

usage example (1): I'm sure we'll be able to get a ticket on the airplane. Besides, **if worse comes to worst**, we can always take a train.

translation: I'm sure we'll be able to get a ticket on the airplane. Besides, in the worst possible case, we could always take a train.

usage example (2): I hope I remembered to pack my shoes for my trip! Oh, well. **If worse comes to worst**, I'll just buy some new ones when I arrive.

translation: I hope I remembered to pack my shoes for my trip! Oh, well. In the worst possible case, I'll just buy some new ones when I arrive.

SYNONYM: "If push comes to shove" *exp.*

let someone off the hook (to) *exp.* to release someone of
responsibility.

usage example (1): I know you broke my watch by accident, so I'm going **to let you off the hook**. Just be careful next time.

translation: I know you broke my watch by accident, so I'm not going to hold you responsible. Just be careful next time.

usage example (2): The police officer **let Greg off the hook** because it was Greg's first offense.

translation: The police officer did not charge Greg because it was his first offense.

NOTE: This expression may also be shortened to **to let someone off** *exp.*

usage example: I'll **let you off** this one time.

translation: I'll release you of responsibility this one time.

SYNONYM: **to let someone slide** *exp.*

on second thought *exp.* upon reconsideration.

usage example (1): I think I'll buy this suit right now. **On second thought**, I'd better wait until I have more money.

translation: I think I'll buy this suit right now. Upon reconsideration, I'd better wait until I have more money.

usage example (2): I think I'll go to Paris on my summer vacation. **On second thought**, I'll go to Switzerland.

translation: I think I'll go to Paris on my summer vacation. Upon reconsideration, I'll go to Switzerland.

Practice the Vocabulary

(Answers to Lesson 3, p. 260)

A. Fill in the blank with the corresponding letter of the word that best completes the phrase.

1. Don't worry. I'm sure Ed will handle the situation calmly. He has a good _____ on his shoulders.
   a. **neck**   b. **head**   c. **clavicle**

2. You're going to have to tell your father that you wrecked his car. There he is now! I guess it's time to _____ the music.
   a. **neck**   b. **mouth**   c. **face**

3. When are you going to _____ the news to your sister that her cat ran away?
   a. **break**   b. **fracture**   c. **smash**

4. I hope we don't miss our bus. I suppose if worse comes to _____ , we can always leave tomorrow instead.
   a. **worse**   b. **worst**   c. **worsen**

5. I was ready to confront him but when I saw how big he was, I got cold _____.
   a. **teeth**   b. **arms**   c. **feet**

6. I'll let you off the _____ this time. But I hope this is the last time you ever forget one of our appointments.
   a. **hook**   b. **look**   c. **book**

7. You've got to come _____ with me and tell me what happened.
   a. **dirty**   b. **filthy**   c. **clean**

8. How much money did you _____ over for that jacket?
   a. **spoon**   b. **fork**   c. **knife**

9. Let's go to the movies. On second _____, let's go bowling.
   a. **thought**   b. **idea**   c. **opinion**

10. Bob got so angry yesterday. I've never seen him fly off the _____ like that before!
    a. **handle**   b. **knob**   c. **dial**

B. Complete the phrases by choosing the appropriate idiom from the list below.

break the news	**if worse comes to worst**
cold feet	**off the hook**
come clean	**on second thought**
face the music	**to fly off the handle**
head on his shoulders	**to fork over**

1. I won't get angry as long as you _____ with me. Are you the one who took my bicycle this morning?

2. I'm going to buy this blue dress. _____ , I think I'll buy the red one instead.

3. I'm sure the cake you're baking will be perfect. Besides, _____ _____ we can always buy one at the market.

4. I should have been home an hour ago. I know my mother's going _____ as soon as I walk in the door. Well, I guess I'd better _____ .

5. I know I said I was going to the singing audition today, but I got _____ .

6. Jack knew exactly what to do after our car accident. He certainly has a good _____ .

7. I'll let you _____ . But if you ever disobey me again, you're going to be in big trouble.

8. Did you _____ to your sister yet about her car being stolen?

9. I can't believe how much money you had _____ for that old car! I think you were overcharged.

C. CONTEXT EXERCISE
Replace the word(s) in italics on the left with the correct phrase from the column on the right.

1. Let's go to the movies. *Upon*

   reconsideration, _____

   _____ I've already

   been to the movies twice this week.

   A. let you off the hook

   B. break the news

   C. face the music

2. Andy was honest with me and

   admitted _____

   that he stole my wallet.

   D. if worse comes to worst

   E. came clean

3. *In the worst possible case,*

   _____

   we can leave tomorrow instead of

   today.

   F. to fork over

   G. on second thought

4. *I'm scared* _____

   _____ .

   H. I've got cold feet

5. You have to be honest with him.   A. **let you off the hook**

It's time to *confront this*

*unpleasant situation*_____

_____ .   B. **break the news**

                      C. **face the music**

6. Did your father *forgive you*

_____

for ruining his car? I've never   D. **if worse comes to worst**

seen anyone so angry before!

                      E. **came clean**

7. Who's going to _____

_____ to Ed

that his car was stolen?   F. **to fork over**

8. Your television set is broken   G. **on second thought**

again? How much did you have

to pay _____ for

that, anyway?   H. **I've got cold feet**

D. WORD SEARCH

Circle the words in the grid (on the opposite page) that complete the following idiomatic expressions. Words may be spelled up, down or diagonally. The first one has been done for you.

1. **"if worse comes to** _____ **"** *exp.* "In the worst possible case."

2. _____ **the news to someone (to)** *exp.* to disclose sensitive and emotional information to someone.

3. **cold** _____ **(to get)** *exp.* to become cowardly and scared.

4. **come** _____ **(to)** *exp.* to be honest (and confess the truth).

5. **face the** _____ **(to)** *exp.* to confront an uncomfortable situation.

6. **fly off the** _____ **(to)** exp. to lose one's temper.

7. _____ **over (to)** *exp.* to pay for something.

8. **have a good head on one's** _____ **(to)** *exp.* said of someone who is very intelligent and rational.

9. **let someone off the** _____ **(to)** *exp.* to release someone of a responsibility.

10. **on second** _____ *exp.* upon reconsideration.

WORD SEARCH

```
N  A  R  K  O  W  M  U  S  I  C  N  A  B
T  B  G  B  U  B  B  L  T  B  T  U  B  R
H  U  C  O  H  C  H  C  K  R  C  E  T  E
O  C  O  D  X  O  A  R  W  C  L  B  D  A
U  K  I  E  S  H  O  U  L  D  E  R  S  K
G  L  O  O  N  F  F  K  G  B  A  N  F  F
H  A  N  D  L  E  L  F  G  C  N  K  U  F
T  L  C  O  V  E  R  H  B  H  K  E  E  E
F  P (W  O  R  S  T) T  L  E  B  U  T  E
E  R  P  J  P  U  S  H  E  R  J  L  P  T
```

E. DICTATION 📼
Test Your Oral Comprehension
(This dictation can be found in Appendix A on page 276).

If you are following along with your cassette, you will now hear a paragraph containing many of the idioms from this section. The paragraph will be read by a native speaker at normal conversational speed (which may seem fast to you at first). In addition, the words will be pronounced *as you would actually hear them in a conversation,* including many common reductions.

The first time the paragraph is presented, simply listen in order to get accustomed to the speed and heavy use of reductions. The paragraph will then be read again with a pause after each group of words to give you time to write down what you heard. The third time the paragraph is read, follow along with what you have written.

How can you say that?!
"Bite your tongue!"

Lesson Four - POPULAR IDIOMS

"Bite your tongue!"

DIALOGUE

Janet sees Anne's triplets for the first time.

Janet: Are these your triplets? They're beautiful! I've seen other babies who were **nothing but skin and bones** at their age. You know, they're the **spitting image** of you and John! Are you planning on having any more?

Anne: **Bite your tongue**! I'm already **at the end of my rope**. Some nights I don't **sleep a wink**. John manages to **sleep like a log** even when the babies are **screaming at the top of their lungs**.

Janet: Well, tell me. How was the labor and delivery?

Anne: I wouldn't say that I **had the time of my life** but at least everything went **without a hitch**.

Janet: Well, **hang in there**. In twenty years, you'll feel it was well worth it!

Lesson Four - POPULAR IDIOMS

Translation of dialogue  in standard English

DIALOGUE

Janet sees Anne's triplets for the first time.

Janet: Are these your triplets? They're beautiful! I've seen other babies who were **extremely thin** at their age. You know, they're **absolutely identical** to you and John! Are you planning on having any more?

Anne: **Stop saying such things**! I'm already **at the limit of what I can tolerate**. Some nights I don't **sleep at all**. John manages to **sleep deeply** even when the babies are **screaming as loudly as they can**.

Janet: Well, tell me. How was the labor and delivery?

Anne: I wouldn't say that I **had the best possible time** but at least everything went **without any problems**.

Janet: Well, **don't give up**. In twenty years, you'll feel it was well worth it!

Lesson Four - POPULAR IDIOMS

Dialogue in slang as it would be heard

"Bite ch'r tongue!"

DIALOGUE

Janet sees Anne's triplets fer the firs' time.

Janet: Are these yer triplets? They're beaudif'l! I've seen other babies who were **nothing b't skin 'n bones** at their age. Ya know, they're the **spit 'n image**'v you 'n John! Are you planning on having any more?

Anne: **Bite ch'r tongue**! I'm already **at the end 'a my rope**. Some nights I don't **sleep a wink**. John manages ta **sleep like a log** even when the babies 'r **screaming at the top 'a their lungs**.

Janet: Well, tell me. How was the labor 'n delivery?

Anne: I wouldn' say thad I **had the time 'a my life** bud 'it least ev'rything went **withoudda hitch**.

Janet: Well, **hang in there**. In twen'y years, you'll feel it was well worth it!

Vocabulary

at the end of one's rope (to be) *exp.* to be at the limit of what
one can tolerate.

usage example (1): I've taken my car to the mechanic five times this
month and it just stopped working again. I'm **at the
end of my rope**!

translation: I've taken my car to the mechanic five times this
month and it just stopped working again. I can't
tolerate it any more.

It was only Monday and Irv was already
"at the end of his rope."

usage example (2): I've tried everything to solve this problem but I just can't find a solution. I'm **at the end of my rope**.

translation: I've tried everything to solve this problem but I just can't find a solution. I'm at the limit of what I can tolerate.

at the top of one's lungs (to scream) *exp.* to scream as loudly as one can.

usage example (1): When Cecily saw the attacker, she **screamed at the top of her lungs**. Luckily, that scared him away.

translation: When Cecily saw the attacker, she screamed as loudly as she could. Luckily, that scared him away.

usage example (2): The music at the party was so loud that we all had **to scream at the top of their lungs**.

translation: The music at the party was so loud that we all had to scream as loudly as we could.

NOTE: Any synonym of the verb "to scream" could be used in this expression such as "to yell," "to shout," "to holler," etc.

bite one's tongue (to) *exp.* (figurative) to keep oneself from verbally attacking someone.

usage example (1): Our new client is so arrogant and insulting, I have to **bite my tongue** around her.

translation: Our new client is so arrogant and insulting, I have to stop myself from verbally attacking her.

usage example (2): If the boss says something you don't like during the meeting, **bite your tongue** or you may get fired!

translation: If the boss says something you don't like during the meeting, stop yourself from verbally attacking him you may get fired!

ALSO: **"Bite your tongue!"** *exp.* "Don't even suggest the possibility of something so dreadful happening!"

usage example: "Your house guest may never leave."
"Bite your tongue!"

translation: "Your house guest may never leave."
"Don't even suggest the possibility of something so dreadful happening!"

go [off] without a hitch (to) *exp.* said of a project or event that proceeds smoothly.

usage example (1): Last night was the first time I ever made dinner for my entire family. I have to admit that it went **[off] without a hitch**.

translation: Last night was the first time I ever made dinner for my entire family. I have to admit that there were no problems at all.

usage example (2): I hope my party **goes without a hitch** tomorrow.

translation: I hope there are no problems at my party tomorrow.

SYNONYM: to go without a snag *exp.* [*"snag"* = (lit); a break or tear in fabric].

hang in there (to) *exp.* • **1.** to wait patiently • **2.** to be strong and persevere.

usage example (1): I'll be over to get you in about an hour, so just **hang in there**.

translation: I'll be over to get you in about an hour, so just wait patiently.

usage example (2): Don't worry. Our aerobics class is almost over. **Hang in there** another five minutes.

translation: Don't worry. Our aerobics class is almost over. Be strong and persevere another five minutes.

have the time of one's life (to) *exp.* to have the best time in one's life.

usage example (1): I had **the time of my life** at your party last night!

translation: I had the best time ever at your party last night!

usage example (2): We had **the time of our lives** yesterday at the amusement park!

translation: We had the best time ever at the amusement park!

The employees at Burke & Burke are having **"the time of their lives"** now that the boss is on vacation!

nothing but skin and bones (to be) *exp.* to be excessively thin.

usage example (1): You're **nothing but skin and bones**! Eat something!

translation: You're so thin! Haven't you been eating well?

usage example (2): He's lost so much weight on his new diet that now he's **nothing but skin and bones**.

translation: He's lost so much weight on his new diet that now he's excessively thin.

sleep a wink (not to) *exp.* not to sleep at all.

usage example (1): I didn't **sleep a wink** last night.

    translation: I didn't sleep at all last night.

usage example (2): The neighbors were making so much noise last night that I didn't **sleep a wink**.

    translation: The neighbors were making so much noise last night that I didn't sleep at all.

sleep like a log (to) *exp.* to sleep soundly.

usage example (1): I **slept like a log** last night.

    translation: I slept soundly last night.

usage example (2): I was awake all night worrying about work but George **slept like a log**.

    translation: I was awake all night worrying about work but George slept soundly.

spitting image of someone (to be the) *exp.* to be identical to someone.

usage example (1): She's the **spitting image** of her mother.

    translation: She looks just like her mother.

usage example (2): They're the **spitting image** of each other.

    translation: They're identical to each other.

    NOTE: This expression is commonly pronounced *"to be the spit'n image of someone."*

  VARIATION: **to be the spit and image of someone** *exp.*

      usage example: He's the **spit and image** of his father.

      translation: He looks just like his father.

Practice the Vocabulary

(Answers to Lesson 4, p. 261)

A. CROSSWORD
Fill in the crossword puzzle on the opposite page by choosing the correct word(s) from the list below.

hang	skin and bones
hitch	spitting
like a log	time
lungs	tongue
rope	wink

Across

4. Our theater production went without a _____ . We didn't have a single problem!

13. Your daughter is the _____ image of you!

17. My throat is sore today. Yesterday we all went to a football game and screamed at the top of our _____ .

22. Bite your _____ ! How could you say such a thing?

25. I feel so rested. I slept _____ last night.

Down

7. I know you're not enjoying your house guest, but just try to _____ in there for one more day. He leaves tomorrow.

9. Have you been on a diet? You're nothing but _____ !

12. I didn't sleep a _____ all night. I was worrying about my English test.

18. My dog ran away yesterday and I've tried everything I can to find him. I'm at the end of my _____ .

24. We had the _____ of our lives at your party last night.

CROSSWORD PUZZLE

B. Choose the phrase that best fits the idiom.

1. You're **nothing but skin and bones**.
   - ☐ a. Have you been sick?
   - ☐ b. Have you been overeating?
   - ☐ c. You must be sleeping well.

2. **Hang in there**!
   - ☐ a. Have you been sick?
   - ☐ b. You look so well rested!
   - ☐ c. The office will close in one hour and you can go home.

3. I had **the time of my life** at Bob's house.
   - ☐ a. I never want to go back there again.
   - ☐ b. I'm looking forward to going back there again soon.
   - ☐ c. What a terrible party!

4. **Bite your tongue**!
   - ☐ a. I can't believe how much you look like your father.
   - ☐ b. Everything went so smoothly at work yesterday.
   - ☐ c. How can you say such a thing?

5. Steve is the **spitting image** of his father.
   - ☐ a. Steve looks just like his father.
   - ☐ b. Steve doesn't look at all like his father.
   - ☐ c. Steve drew a picture of his father.

6. I **slept like a log** last night.
   - ☐ a. I hope I don't have another night like that!
   - ☐ b. I'm so tired today.
   - ☐ c. I feel so rested today.

7. I **didn't sleep a wink** last night.
   - ☐ a. I'm exhausted today.
   - ☐ b. I've never slept so well in my life.
   - ☐ c. I feel so rested today.

8. I'm **at the end of my rope**.
   - ☐ a. I can't continue.
   - ☐ b. I'm so happy.
   - ☐ c. I feel so rested today.

C. Complete the dialogue using the appropriate word(s) from the list below.

bite your tongue   **like a log**
end of my rope   **sleep a wink**
hang in there   **the time of my life**
hitch

Debbie: Thank you so much for inviting me to your party. I really had

(1)_____ ! Everything went

without a **(2)**_____ .

Nancy: I know. I didn't think I'd **(3)**_____

_____ the night before. Actually, I slept

(4)_____ ! I guess I was

exhausted from preparing all the food.

Debbie: The last time I had a party, I was at the

(5)_____ ! Nothing went right.

I kept telling myself to **(6)**_____

until everyone went home.

Nancy: I don't suppose you'll be having another party soon?

Debbie: **(7)**_____!

D. CONTEXT EXERCISE
Choose the idiom from the right column that matches the phrase in the left column.

☐ 1. I can't work like this any more. It's just too much for me!

☐ 2. You can certainly tell that Gordon is John's son.

☐ 3. You've got to eat something!

☐ 4. I heard you went skiing for the first time yesterday. Are you going next weekend, too?

☐ 5. I'm so tired.

☐ 6. I can't believe you didn't hear me calling you.

☐ 7. What a great vacation!

☐ 8. I can't wait to go home!

☐ 9. Why are you so worried that your party won't be a success? Everyone is having a great time. Just relax.

☐ 10. I'm very rested.

A. I was **screaming at the top of my lungs**!

B. I'm **at the end of my rope**.

C. **Bite your tongue**! I'm never going again. I spent the whole day falling.

D. He's the **spitting mage** of his father.

E. I had **the time of my life**.

F. I **didn't sleep a wink** all night.

G. You're **nothing but skin and bones**!

H. I **slept like a log** last night.

I. I hope I can **hang in there** another five minutes until the office closes!

J. Everything's going **without a hitch**!

E. DICTATION
Test Your Oral Comprehension
(This dictation can be found in Appendix A on page 277).

If you are following along with your cassette, you will now hear a paragraph containing many of the idioms from this section. The paragraph will be read by a native speaker at normal conversational speed (which may seem fast to you at first). In addition, the words will be pronounced *as you would actually hear them in a conversation,* including many common reductions.

The first time the paragraph is presented, simply listen in order to get accustomed to the speed and heavy use of reductions. The paragraph will then be read again with a pause after each group of words to give you time to write down what you heard. The third time the paragraph is read, follow along with what you have written.

My house guest is
"eating me out of house and home!"

Lesson Five - POPULAR IDIOMS

My house guest is "eating me out of house and home!"

DIALOGUE

Jim is having trouble with his house guest.

Emily: Are things still going badly with your house guest?

Jim: It's getting worse. Now he's **eating me out of house and home**. I've tried talking to him but **it all goes in one ear and out the other**. He **makes himself at home** which is fine. But **what really gets me** is that yesterday he walked into the living room **in the raw** and I had company over! That was **the last straw**.

Emly: Jim, I really think you're **beating around the bush** with this guy. I know he used to be your best friend in college, but I really think it's time **to lay down the law**.

Jim: You're right. Everything is probably going **to come to a head** tonight. I'll **keep you posted**.

Lesson Five - POPULAR IDIOMS

Translation of dialogue in standard English

DIALOGUE

Jim is having trouble with his house guest.

Emily: Are things still going badly with your house guest?

Jim: It's getting worse. Now he's **eating everything in my house**. I've tried talking to him but **he doesn't listen**. He **makes himself as comfortable as if he were in his own home** which is fine. But what really **annoys me** is that yesterday he walked into the living room **completely naked** and I had company over! That was **all I could tolerate**.

Emily: Jim, I really think you're **being indirect** with this guy. I know he used to be your best friend in college, but I really think it's time **to impose strict rules**.

Jim: You're right. Everything is probably going **to reach the critical point** tonight. I'll **keep you informed**.

Dialogue in slang as it would be heard

My house guest 'z "eading me oud of house 'n home!"

DIALOGUE

Jim is having trouble with his house guest.

Emily: Are things still going badly with yer house guest?

Jim: It's gedding worse. Now 'e's **eading me oud of house 'n home**. I've tried talking to 'im bud **id all goes 'n one ear 'n out the other**. He **makes 'imself 'it home** which 'z fine. But **what really gets me** is that yesterday 'e walked inta the living room **'n the raw** and I had company over! That was **the las' straw**.

Emily: Jim, I really think y'r **beading aroun' the bush** with this guy. I know 'e used ta be yer bes' friend 'n college, bud I really think it's time **ta lay down the law**.

Jim: Y'r right. Ev'rything is prob'ly gonna **come to a head** t'night. I'll **keep ya posted**.

Vocabulary

beat around the bush (to) *exp.* to be indirect and vague.

> *usage example (1):* Just tell me what you want. Stop **beating around the bush**!
>
> *translation:* Just tell me what you want. Stop being so indirect and vague!
>
> *usage example (2):* Stop **beating around the bush**. If you want to borrow my car, just ask me.
>
> *translation:* Stop being so indirect and vague. If you want to borrow my car, just ask me.

come to a head (to) *exp.* said of a situation which reaches a critical point; to come to a climax.

> *usage example (1):* They've been angry with each other for a long time and last night everything **came to a head**. They yelled at each other for an entire hour!
>
> *translation:* They've been angry with each other for a long time and last night the situation reached a critical point. They yelled at each other for an entire hour!
>
> *usage example (2):* Every time Karen comes to our house, she criticizes me. Well, if she makes any comments about my haircut, things are going **to come to a head**!
>
> *translation:* Every time Karen comes to our house she criticizes me. Well, if she makes any comments about my haircut, things are going to climax!

eat someone out of house and home (to) *exp.* to eat all the food in someone's house to the point where the owners can barely afford to buy more food and other essentials.

usage example (1): My cousin has been staying with us for two months and it's been terrible. He has an enormous appetite. If he stays much longer, he'll **eat us out of house and home**!

translation: My cousin has been staying with us for two months and it's been terrible. He has an enormous appetite. If he stays much longer, we won't be able to afford to live!

usage example (2): My cousin Gary is known for visiting people, **eating them out of house and home**, and never offering to pay for anything.

translation: My cousin Gary is known for visiting people, eating everything in their house, and never offering to pay for anything.

get someone (to) *exp.* to annoy someone.

usage example (1): It really **gets me** when people lie!

translation: It really annoys me when people lie!

usage example (2): Doesn't it **get you** when people are late?

translation: Doesn't it annoy you when people are late?

VARIATION: **to get to someone** *exp.* to annoy or to upset.

usage example: He's starting **to get to me**.

translation: He's starting to annoy (or upset) me.

go in one ear and out the other (to) *exp.* to ignore what someone says; not to pay attention to what someone says.

usage example (1): I've told you three times to take off your shoes before you walk on the new carpet. I feel like everything I say to you **goes in one ear and out the other**.

translation: I've told you three times to take off your shoes before you walk on the new carpet. I feel like you ignore everything I say to you.

usage example (2): I know he can be insulting sometimes. If he says anything rude to you, just let it **go in one ear and out the other**.

translation: I know he can be insulting sometimes. If he says anything rude to you, just ignore it.

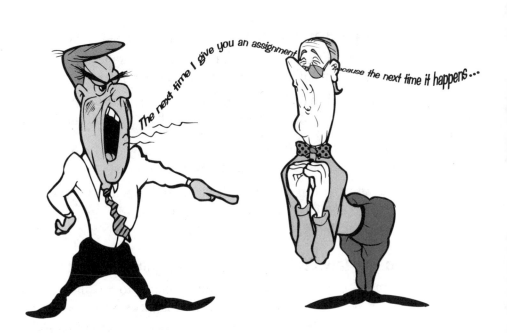

The next time I give you an assignment... because the next time it happens...

Mr. Rodney's problem is that everything "goes in one ear and out the other."

in the raw (to be) *exp.* to be completely naked.

usage example (1): I guess he didn't know I was in the house. When I walked into the living room, he was just standing there **in the raw**!

translation: I guess he didn't know I was in the house. When I walked into the living room, he was just standing there completely naked!

usage example (2): Everyone at this beach is **in the raw**!

translation: Everyone at this beach is completely naked!

SYNONYM: **to be in one's birthday suit** *exp.* (humorous) • (lit); to be dressed the same way as one is at the moment of birth; naked.

keep someone posted (to) *exp.* to keep someone informed.

usage example (1): I'm not sure when I'll be arriving at the airport, but I should know tomorrow. I'll **keep you posted**.

translation: I'm not sure when I'll be arriving at the airport, but I should know tomorrow. I'll keep you informed.

usage example (2): I can't wait to hear what happens on your job interview. **Keep me posted**.

translation: I can't wait to hear what happens on your job interview. Keep me informed.

lay down the law (to) *exp.* to impose strict rules.

usage example (1): I'm tired of you kids coming to my house and misbehaving! Now I'm **laying down the law**. There will be no jumping, no yelling, and no hitting while you're in my home. Is that clear?

translation: I'm tired of you kids coming to my house and misbehaving! Now I'm imposing strict rules. There will be no jumping, no yelling, and no hitting while you're in my home. Is that clear?

usage example (2): The boss **laid down the law** today. Anyone who is late to work will be fired!

translation: The boss imposed strict rules today. Anyone who is late to work will be fired!

make oneself at home (to)   *exp.* to make oneself feel as comfortable as if he/she were in his/her own home.

usage example (1):   Welcome to my house. Please **make yourself at home**.

   translation: Welcome to my house. Please make yourself feel as comfortable as you would in your own home.

usage example (2):   It's hard **to make yourself at home** at Lisa's house because she's so formal.

   translation: It's hard to feel comfortable at Lisa's house because she's so formal.

the last straw (to be) *exp.* to be all one can tolerate.

usage example (1):   Our next door neighbors have been playing loud music since midnight. Now they're throwing empty bottles in our backyard! **That's the last straw**. I'm calling the police.

   translation: Our next door neighbors have been playing loud music since midnight. Now they're throwing empty bottles in our backyard! That's all I'm going to tolerate. I'm calling the police.

usage example (2):   Bob took money out of my wallet without asking? **That's the last straw**!

   translation: Bob took money out of my wallet without asking? That's all I'm going to tolerate!

   VARIATION: **to be the straw that broke the camel's back** *exp.*

Practice the Vocabulary 📼

(Answers to Lesson 5, p. 262)

A. Were the following idioms used correctly or incorrectly?

1. I'm **laying down the law**. These are the new rules in my home.
   ☐ correct   ☐ incorrect

2. I'm not going to give you any information about the situation. **I'll keep you posted**.
   ☐ correct   ☐ incorrect

3. Everything you say to George **goes in one ear and out the other**. He always pays attention to what people say.
   ☐ correct   ☐ incorrect

4. Stop being so indirect and vague. You don't need **to beat around the bush**.
   ☐ correct   ☐ incorrect

5. Did you see that beautiful dress she was wearing? That was the first time I'd ever seen her **in the raw**.
   ☐ correct   ☐ incorrect

6. It really **gets me** when people lie. Why can't people just tell the truth!
   ☐ correct   ☐ incorrect

7. Everything finally **came to a head** last night. You should have heard them yell at each other!
   ☐ correct   ☐ incorrect

8. Take off your coat and **make yourself at home**. Please help yourself to something to drink.
   ☐ correct   ☐ incorrect

B. Underline the appropriate word that best completes the phrase.

1. You never listen to me. It all goes in one (**arm**, **ear**, **mouth**) and out the other.

2. Stop (**hitting**, **beating**, **whipping**) around the bush and tell me what you want.

3. Everything came to a (**foot**, **head**, **leg**) last night between Steve and Ron. You should have heard them yell at each other.

4. That's the last (**straw**, **hay**, **grass**)! I'm going to quit my job!

5. My house guest is eating me out of house and (**home**, **dwelling**, **abode**)!

6. Make yourself at (**house**, **home**, **dwelling**). I'll be right back with some refreshments.

7. I can't wait to hear what happens on your vacation. Keep me (**posted**, **roasted**, **toasted**).

8. Nancy's late for our appointment again. That really (**gets**, **bets**, **sets**) me.

C. Choose the most appropriate definition of the words in boldface.

1. I've tried talking to him but **it all goes in one ear and out the other**.
   - ☐ a. he doesn't pay attention
   - ☐ b. he gets very defensive
   - ☐ c. his hearing is very bad

2. You children have to learn to behave. Starting today, I'm **laying down the law**.
   - ☐ a. going to keep you informed
   - ☐ b. going to be indirect and vague
   - ☐ c. imposing strict rules

3. I'm going to find out what the problem is with Stephanie. She seems very upset. I'll **keep you posted**.
   - ☐ a. keep you informed
   - ☐ b. be indirect and vague
   - ☐ c. impose strict rules

4. Stop **beating around the bush** and tell me what you want.
   - ☐ a. keeping me informed
   - ☐ b. being indirect and vague
   - ☐ c. imposing strict rules

5. Everyone in the swimming pool was **in the raw**.
   - ☐ a. fully clothed
   - ☐ b. slowly
   - ☐ c. nude

6. There's so much tension between Jan and John. I think it's all going to **come to a head** tonight.
   - ☐ a. calm down
   - ☐ b. climax
   - ☐ c. end

7. **Make yourself at home** and I'll be right back with some food.
   - ☐ a. make yourself as comfortable as you would in your own home
   - ☐ b. don't touch anything in my home
   - ☐ c. take anything you'd like from my home

8. What really **gets me** is that every time I say hello to Al, he ignores me.
   - ☐ a. makes me laugh
   - ☐ b. annoys me
   - ☐ c. relaxes me

9. That's **the last straw**! I'm leaving!
   - ☐ a. all I can tolerate
   - ☐ b. wonderful
   - ☐ c. exciting

10. Jack's brother is **eating us out of house and home**.
    - ☐ a. eating very little
    - ☐ b. eating only sweets
    - ☐ c. eating everything in our house

D. CONTEXT EXERCISE
Choose the correct idiom that goes with the phrase.

1. Today I'm going to find out if I got the job promotion.
   - ☐ a. **I'll keep you posted.**
   - ☐ b. **Make yourself at home.**

2. Did you see how pretentious Anne was at the party?
   - ☐ a. **That really gets me.**
   - ☐ b. **I'm laying down the law.**

3. You should have heard their argument!
   - ☐ a. **It finally came to a head last night.**
   - ☐ b. **I'm laying down the law.**

4. Tell me what really happened!
   □ a. **It's all going in one ear and out the other!**
   □ b. **Stop beating around the bush!**

5. I've gone to the market three times today.
   □ a. **My son is eating us out of house and home.**
   □ b. **My son keeps beating around the bush.**

6. He doesn't hear a word I say.
   □ a. **Everything goes in one ear and out the other.**
   □ b. **He keeps beating around the bush.**

7. This is my first time to a nudist colony.
   □ a. **He's eating me out of house and home.**
   □ b. **I think we're the only people who aren't in the raw.**

8. I told you to come home before midnight and now it's 2:00 in the morning!
   □ a. **That's the last straw!**
   □ b. **Stop beating around the bush!**

E. DICTATION
Test Your Oral Comprehension
(This dictation can be found in Appendix A on page 277).

If you are following along with your cassette, you will now hear a paragraph containing many of the idioms from this section. The paragraph will be read by a native speaker at normal conversational speed (which may seem fast to you at first). In addition, the words will be pronounced *as you would actually hear them in a conversation,* including many common reductions.

The first time the paragraph is presented, simply listen in order to get accustomed to the speed and heavy use of reductions. The paragraph will then be read again with a pause after each group of words to give you time to write down what you heard. The third time the paragraph is read, follow along with what you have written.

REVIEW EXAM FOR LESSONS 1-5

(Answers to Review, p. 263)

A. Underline the appropriate word that best completes the phrase.

1. I had the time of my (**life, death, sleep**) at your party last night.

2. When you said she was pretentious, you hit the nail on the (**foot, head, arm**).

3. You don't know why she's so upset? It's as plain as the (**eye, mouth, nose**) on your face.

4. Mark's car was stolen from his house while he was on vacation! I don't know how I'm going to (**break, smash, crush**) the news to him.

5. Don't worry about missing the flight. If worse comes to (**worst, better, best**), we'll leave tomorrow.

6. Laura is dating Ralph? You're pulling my (**arm, leg, ear**)!

7. Janet's relationship with Ernie is nothing more than a flash in the (**casserole, pot, pan**).

8. They must be good friends. I saw them walking arm in (**foot, finger, arm**) yesterday.

9. When the teacher gave us a surprise exam, I broke out in a (**warm, cold, hot**) sweat.

10. There's nothing to get so upset about. You're really (**blowing, breathing, rowing**) this all out of proportion.

B. CROSSWORD

Step 1: Fill in the blanks with the appropriate word(s) from the list below.

Step 2: Using your answers, fill in the crossword puzzle on page 81.

a hold of yourself	flash	leg
break	fork	lungs
clean	gets	raw
cold sweat	handle	sight
cradle	hang in there	skin and bones
deep	hitch	spit
fair shake	knot	straw
feet	law	tune

Across

1. You've got to get _____ . I've never seen you so upset.

7. I know you want Joanne to be your girlfriend, but there's just one _____ . I just found out she's married.

8. Mark is going to be so upset when I tell him about his house burning in the fire today. I don't know how I'm going to _____ the news to him.

9. You broke my good watch? That's the last _____ ! I'm never letting you borrow anything of mine again!

10. You're twenty years older than your boyfriend? People are going to say that you're robbing the _____ .

Across (continued)

11. You found $1,000? Your pulling my _____ !

12. I know she's lied to you before, but I think she's ready to come _____ with you this time.

13. Our flight to Los Angeles was very expensive. We had to _____ over a lot of money.

15. When her cat died, Pam went off the _____ end.

16. I was so scared I broke out in a _____ .

20. Congratulations! I just heard you and Colby are going to tie the _____ ! I hope you have a long and happy life together.

21. Put something on before our company gets here. I don't think they're interested in seeing you in the _____ .

22. Dan was going to get married yesterday but he got cold _____ and cancelled the ceremony.

23. David flew off the _____ because Keith was late again. That always makes David angry.

24. You know what really _____ me? It took me three months to find a job but my sister found one in only an hour and it pays twice as much as mine!

Down

2. I know you have a lot of work to do, but _____ . When it's all done, you can take a long vacation.

3. When Karen saw the burglers, she screamed at the top of her _____ and scared them away.

4. My job interview only lasted two minutes. I wasn't given a _____ .

5. John lost a lot of weight. He's nothing but _____ .

6. Kelly was a movie star for a short time. Her career was only a _____ in the pan.

14. Amy is the _____ and image of her mother. You can certainly see that they're related.

17. You're three hours late coming home! I'm laying down the _____ right now. If you ever come this late again, I'm taking away your privileges.

18. When I met your mother, it was love at first _____ . I knew I wanted to spend the rest of my life with her.

19. I can carry a _____ although I wouldn't call myself a great singer.

CROSSWORD PUZZLE

C. TRUE or FALSE
Are the following sentences (containing idiomatic expressions) true or false?

1. The best singer in the world can't **carry a tune**.
   ☐ True   ☐ False

2. After someone **pops the question**, hopefully the next step is **to tie the knot**.
   ☐ True   ☐ False

3. Only brave people get **cold feet**.
   ☐ True   ☐ False

4. When you **come clean** with someone, you're not being honest.
   ☐ True   ☐ False

5. If you are the **spitting image** of someone, you look alike.
   ☐ True   ☐ False

6. When something goes without a **hitch**, it means that everything went smoothly.
   ☐ True   ☐ False

7. Fat people are **nothing but skin and bones**.
   ☐ True   ☐ False

8. People who never get angry are known for **flying off the handle**.
   ☐ True   ☐ False

9. If you have insomnia, you probably **sleep like a log**.
   ☐ True   ☐ False

10. If you have insomnia, you probably can't **sleep a wink**.
   ☐ True   ☐ False

D. CONTEXT EXERCISE
Choose the idiom from the right column that goes with the phrase in the left column.

☐ 1. I wonder if Mark and Angie will be getting married soon.

☐ 2. You're dating someone twenty years younger than you?

☐ 3. Peter is always very rational.

☐ 4. Andy was arrested last night for drunk driving, but they let him go home after an hour.

☐ 5. Let's go to the movies.

☐ 6. Thank you for inviting me to your party last night. Are you going to have another party next weekend, too?

☐ 7. You look tired today.

☐ 8. You have a beautiful house!

☐ 9. Do you think the boss will give me a promotion next week?

☐ 10. I've never seen you so upset and irrational.

A. That's right. People are going to say that I'm **robbing the cradle**.

B. I didn't **sleep a wink** last night.

C. Great! **On second thought**, let's go get something to eat. I don't feel like sitting in a dark theater all night.

D. They **let him off the hook** that quickly?

E. **Bite your tongue**! I'm exhausted.

F. Are you serious? You don't have a **prayer**.

G. Thank you. **Make yourself at home**.

H. That's true. He really **has a good head on his shoulders**.

I. No, they've only been **going together** for a week!

J. You're right. I've got to **get a hold of myself**.

A "bad hair" day...

Lesson Six - POPULAR IDIOMS

Dialogue In Slang

"A bad hair day"

DIALOGUE

Scott and Sabrina are at a party.

Scott: Wow! Emily really **went to town** on this party. Oh, I think that's a **no-host bar**. I hope you brought money, because I didn't.

Sabrina: Oh, sure. No problem. Hey, look who just walked in. I didn't know Barbara was going to be here. Is she **having a bad hair day** or what? I've never seen hair that color before! Even getting **all dolled up** isn't going to help her. I don't mean **to get on her case** but I've never met anyone who can **get on my nerves** like she can!

Scott: I know. She's always **making cracks** about everyone **behind their backs**. Oh, great. Here she comes. Whatever you do, don't **buy into it** when she starts **fishing for compliments** about how good she looks.

Sabrina: I don't think there's much chance of that happening.

Lesson Six - POPULAR IDIOMS

Translation of  dialogue in standard English

DIALOGUE

Scott and Sabrina are at a party.

Scott: Wow! Emily really **spent a lot of money** on this party. Oh, I think that's a **bar where we pay for our own drinks**. I hope you brought money, because I didn't.

Sabrina: Oh, sure. No problem. Hey, look who just walked in. I didn't know Barbara was going to be here. Does her **hair look terrible** or what? I've never seen hair that color before! Even getting **dressed in attractive clothing** isn't going to help her. I don't mean **to criticize her** but I've never met anyone who can **annoy me** like she can!

Scott: I know. She's always **making derogatory remarks** about everyone **without their knowledge and in a malicious way**. Oh, great. Here she comes. Whatever you do, don't **be tricked** into **complimenting her** about how good she looks.

Sabrina: I don't think there's much chance of that happening.

Lesson Six - POPULAR IDIOMS

Dialogue in slang as it would be heard

"A bad hair day"

DIALOGUE

Scott 'n Sabrina 'r ad a pardy.

Scott: Wow! Emily really **went ta town** on this pardy. Oh, I think that's a **no-host bar**. I hope you brought money, 'cause I didn't.

Sabrina: Oh, sh'r. No problem. Hey, look 'oo jus' walked in. I didn' know Barb'ra was gonna be here. Ishee **having a bad hair day** 'r what? I've never seen hair that color b'fore! Even gedding **all dolled up** isn't gonna help her. I don' mean **ta ged on 'er case** bud I've never med anyone who c'n **ged on my nerves** like she can!

Scott: I know. She's always **making cracks** aboud ev'ryone **b'hin' their backs**. Oh, great. Here she comes. Whadever ya do, don't **buy into it** when she starts **fishing fer compliments** about how good she looks.

Sabrina: I don' think there's much chance 'a that happ'ning.

Vocabulary

bad hair day (to have a) *exp.* (very popular) said of someone whose hair looks messy or poorly styled.

    usage example (1): I can't be seen in public today. I'm **having a bad hair day**.

        translation: I can't be seen in public today. My hair looks absolutely terrible.

    usage example (2): I can't believe this. I'm going to be on television for the first time in my life and I'm **having a bad hair day**!

        translation: I can't believe this. I'm going to be on television for the first time in my life and my hair looks terrible!

    ANTONYM: **to have a good hair day** *exp.*

behind someone's back (to do something) *exp.* to do something secretly and in a malicious manner.

    usage example (1): I just found out that Todd's been talking about me **behind my back**.

        translation: I just found out that Todd's been secretly talking about me in a malicious manner.

    usage example (2): We agreed that we were going to apply for the job as a team, but you went **behind my back**!

        translation: We agreed that we were going to apply for the job as a team, but you went and applied without telling me!

buy into something (to) *exp.* to accept something.

    usage example (1): He gave you nothing but excuses and you **bought into it**!

> Don't look, but guess who just walked in... Barbara. I don't mean **to talk about her behind her back**, but is she ever **having a bad hair day!**

translation: He gave you nothing but excuses and you accepted it!

usage example (2): She's going to try to make you feel guilty if you don't agree to take her to the airport. Just don't **buy into it**!

translation: She's going to try to make you feel guilty if you don't agree to take her to the airport. Just don't accept that!

SYNONYM: **to fall for something** *exp.*

usage example: Why do you keep falling for his excuses?

translation: Why do you keep accepting his excuses?

dolled up (to get all) *exp.* to get all dressed up.

usage example (1):   I told her that we were only going to a barbecue but
                        she still wanted **to get all dolled up**.

translation: I told her that we were only going to a barbecue but
                  she still wanted to get all dressed up.

usage example (2):   You didn't need **to get all dolled up** for my party. I
                        told you it was going to be very casual.

translation: You didn't need to get all dressed up for my party. I
                  told you it was going to be very casual.

NOTE: This expression is used to describe women only. For
             both men and women, a common expression is:
             to get all decked out.

SYNONYM: **to be dressed to kill** *exp.* to be dressed beautifully
                (may be applied to both men and women).

usage example: Laura was **dressed to kill** tonight!

translation: Laura was all dressed up tonight!

Miss Jones got "all dolled up" for her first day at Rosenchumps, Liar, & Susspool.

fish for a compliment from someone (to) *exp.* to try and get a
compliment from someone.

usage example (1): Today Lauren showed me one of the paintings she
made. You should have heard her talk for an hour
about what a great job she did. She was definitely
fishing for a compliment.

translation: Today Lauren showed me one of the paintings she
made. You should have heard her talk for an hour
about what a great job she did. She was definitely
trying to get me to compliment her.

usage example (2): Carol invited some of us over for dinner last night. It
was the worst food I've ever tasted. She kept **fishing
for compliments** about the meal but no one could say
anything positive.

translation: Carol invited some of us over for dinner last night. It
was the worst food I've ever tasted. She kept trying
to get compliments for the meal but no one could say
anything positive.

get on someone's case (to) *exp.* to criticize someone.

usage example (1): Why do you always have **to get on my case** every
time I make a little mistake?

translation: Why do you always have to criticize me every time I
make a little mistake?

usage example (2): My mom really **got on my case** for being late to
dinner.

translation: My mom really criticized me for being late to dinner.

get on someone's nerves (to) *exp.* to annoy someone.

usage example (1): That loud music is **getting on my nerves**!

translation: That loud music is annoying me!

usage example (2): Would you please leave me alone! You're starting **to get on my nerves**!

translation: Would you please leave me alone! You're starting to annoy me!

go to town (to) *exp.* to do something to the extreme.

usage example (1): That saxophonist really **went to town** on his solo!

translation: That saxophonist really played his solo with complete abandon!

usage example (2): Michelle hired a band, a caterer, and even rented tables and chairs for her party. Every time she gives a party, she always **goes to town**.

translation: Michelle hired a band, a caterer, and even rented tables and chairs for her party. Every time she gives a party, she always does it as elaborately as possible.

SYNONYM (1): **to go all out** *exp.*

usage example: You really **went all out** for this party!

translation: You really spared no expense for this party!

SYNONYM (2): **to let out all the stops** *exp.*

usage example: When Joanne gives a party, she **lets out all the stops!**

translation: When Joanne has a party, she goes all the way!

make cracks about someone or something (to) *exp.* to make derogatory remarks about someone or something.

usage example (1): If you **make another crack** about my best friend, I'll never speak to you again.

translation: If you make another derogatory remark about my best friend, I'll never speak to you again.

usage example (2):   Jody **made cracks** about Nancy all night. When I finally told Jody that Nancy was my sister, you should have seen her face!

translation: Jody made derogatory remarks about Nancy all night. When I finally told Jody that Nancy was my sister, you should have seen her face!

no-host bar *exp.* a bar at a party where the guests are expected to pay for their drinks.

usage example (1):   If you want something to drink, you'll have to pay for it. It's a **no-host bar**.

translation: If you want something to drink, you'll have to pay for it. The guests have to pay for their own drinks.

usage example (2):   I want to have a huge party but I'm going to have to set up a **no-host bar**. I wouldn't be able to afford to buy liquor for that many people.

translation: I want to have a huge party but I'm going to have to set up a bar where the guests pay for their own drinks. I wouldn't be able to afford to buy liquor for that many people.

NOTE: The term *"no-host"* bar is only common in the western portion of the United States, whereas the expression *"cash-bar"* is used in the east.

Practice The Vocabulary

(Answers to Lesson 6, p. 264)

A. Were the idioms in the following sentences used correctly or incorrectly?

1. It's time to go to bed. I'm going **to get all dolled up**.
   ☐ correct   ☐ incorrect

2. Janet really **went to town** on this party! She probably didn't spend any money on it at all!
   ☐ correct   ☐ incorrect

3. You're **getting on my nerves**. Go away!
   ☐ correct   ☐ incorrect

4. My mother **gets on my case** every time I spend a lot of money.
   ☐ correct   ☐ incorrect

5. Matt was **making cracks about** Erica at the party last night. He must really admire her a lot.
   ☐ correct   ☐ incorrect

6. Make sure you bring money with you to the party. There's going to be a **no-host bar**.
   ☐ correct   ☐ incorrect

7. I'm having a **bad hair day**. I look terrible!
   ☐ correct   ☐ incorrect

8. Ernie gets so embarrassed anytime someone gives him any praise. I guess that's why he's always **fishing for compliments**.
   ☐ correct   ☐ incorrect

B. Choose the correct answer from the list below.

a bad hair day   getting on your nerves
all dolled up   getting on your case
behind my back   making cracks about him/her
buying into it   no-host
fishing for compliments   to go to town

1. Someone whose hair looks terrible is said to be having:

   Answer: _____

2. What is an idiom for doing something to the extreme?

   Answer: _____

3. If people are making derogatory comments about me that I am
   unaware of, they are talking:

   Answer: _____

4. A woman who is wearing beautiful clothing is:

   Answer: _____

5. When someone annoys you, he/she is:

   Answer: _____

6. When someone wants to be praised, he/she is:

   Answer: _____

7. If you are saying something derogatory about a particular person, you are said to be:

Answer: _____

8. A bar where guests are expected to pay for their drinks is what kind of bar?

Answer: _____

9. If you are accepting someone's excuse, you are:

Answer: _____

10. If someone cricitizes you, he/she is:

Answer: _____

C. Underline the appropriate word that best completes the phrase.

1. He loves when people praise him. He's always (**bowling, fishing, skiing**) for compliments.

2. Marge really went to (**town, city, village**) on her house. It's beautiful!

3. Barbara just walked in. I hope she doesn't come and sit with us. She really gets on my (**muscles, cells, nerves**).

4. You should have heard what Ted said about you behind your (**ear, back, neck**).

5. Why are you all dolled (**up, down, back**)? Are you on your way to a party?

6. If Anna starts hinting that she needs a ride to the airport, don't (**purchase, spend, buy**) into it.

7. I can't go to the party looking like this. I'm having a bad hair (**day, night, week**).

8. Stop getting on my (**case, suitcase, valise**). You're always criticizing me!

9. We have to pay for our own drinks. It's a (**yes, no, maybe**)-host bar.

10. Stop making (**cracks, crevices, splits**) about my girlfriend!

D. Choose the correct definition of the idioms in boldface.

1. Donna is wearing the ugliest dress today but she must think it's beautiful. She's been **fishing for compliments** all day.
   ☐ a. accepting compliments
   ☐ b. looking for compliments
   ☐ c. giving compliments

2. My mother got **all dolled up** to go to her high school reunion.
   ☐ a. completely drunk
   ☐ b. in old clothes
   ☐ c. dressed in formal clothing

3. Every time I'm late to work, my boss **gets on my case**.
   ☐ a. criticizes me
   ☐ b. doesn't care
   ☐ c. thinks it's funny

4. Joanne keeps **making cracks** about the way I dress.
   ☐ a. making helpful comments
   ☐ b. making derogatory comments
   ☐ c. insightful comments

5. I'm **having a bad hair day**.
   ☐ a. having trouble with my hair today
   ☐ b. not having any trouble with my hair today
   ☐ c. beautiful with my new hairdo

6. That customer always **gets on my nerves**.
   ☐ a. has something nice to say
   ☐ b. makes me laugh
   ☐ c. annoys me

7. Don't **buy into it** when Carol asks to borrow money for the bus. She uses that same story with everyone.
   ☐ a. laugh
   ☐ b. accept it
   ☐ c. cry

8. Did you hear what Dave is saying about Eric **behind his back**?
   ☐ a. without his knowledge
   ☐ b. while hiding behind him
   ☐ c. with his knowledge

E. DICTATION
Test Your Oral Comprehension
(This dictation can be found in Appendix A on page 278).

If you are following along with your cassette, you will now hear a paragraph containing many of the idioms from this section. The paragraph will be read by a native speaker at normal conversational speed (which may seem fast to you at first). In addition, the words will be pronounced *as you would actually hear them in a conversation,* including many common reductions.

The first time the paragraph is presented, simply listen in order to get accustomed to the speed and heavy use of reductions. The paragraph will then be read again with a pause after each group of words to give you time to write down what you heard. The third time the paragraph is read, follow along with what you have written.

Jody is "getting the hang of skiing"

Lesson Seven - POPULAR IDIOMS

Jodi is "getting the hang of skiing"

DIALOGUE

Jodi is learning how to ski.

Jodi: I know I'm going **to bite the dust** going down this hill. I had a **brush with death** on the chair lift! This is going to be so embarrassing.

Nancy: Don't worry. Everyone knows you're **getting your feet wet**. I'll show you how. I bet you'll **get the hang** of this within five minutes.

Jodi: This is only your second time skiing. This is definitely a case of **the blind leading the blind**.

Nancy: Relax. I can **hold my own**. Now, point your skis toward the bottom of the hill. **Easy does it**!

Jodi: I don't think I can **get up enough nerve** to do this.

Nancy: Here. I'll just give you a little push...

Jodi: No!!!!!!!!!

(Later at the bottom of the hill...)

Nancy: There. Now, wasn't that fun? As soon as you **get your second wind**, we'll try it again.

Jodi: **Don't hold your breath**!

Lesson Seven - POPULAR IDIOMS

DIALOGUE

Jodi is learning how to ski.

Jodi: I know I'm going **to fall hard** going down this hill. I **almost got killed** on the chair lift! This is going to be so embarrassing.

Nancy: Don't worry. Everyone knows this is your **first experience**. I'll show you how. I bet you'll **be proficient** at this within five minutes.

Jodi: This is only your second time skiing. This is definitely a case of **an inexperienced person being instructed by someone equally inexperienced**.

Nancy: Relax. I'm **very capable**. Now, point your skis toward the bottom of the hill. **Be careful and go slowly**!

Jodi: I don't think I can **get the courage** to do this.

Nancy: Here. I'll just give you a little push...

Jodi: No!!!!!!!!!

(Later at the bottom of the hill...)

Nancy: There. Now, wasn't that fun? As soon as you **get a second burst of energy**, we'll try it again.

Jodi: **Don't anticipate that happening**!

Dialogue in slang as it would be heard

Jodi'z "gedding the hang of skiing"

DIALOGUE

Jodi's learning how da ski.

Jodi: I know I'm gonna **bite the dust** going down this hill. I had a **brush with death** on the chair lift! This is gonna be so embarrassing.

Nancy: Don't worry. Ev'ryone knows y'r **gedding yer feet wet**. I'll show you how. I bet chew'll **get the hang** 'a this within five minutes.

Jodi: This is only yer secon' time skiing. This is definitely a case 'a **the blind leading the blind**.

Nancy: Relax. I c'n **hold my own**. Now, point ch'r skis tord the bodom 'a the hill. **Easy does it**!

Jodi: I don' think I c'n **ged up anuf nerve** ta do this.

Nancy: Here. I'll jus' give you a liddle push...

Jodi: No!!!!!!!!!

(Lader at the bodom 'a the hill...)

Nancy: There. Now, wasn' that fun? As soon 'ez you **get ch'r secon' wind**, we'll try id again.

Jodi: **Don't hold'j'er breath**!

Vocabulary

bite the dust (to) *exp.* • **1.** to fall (on the ground, looking as if one is eating dust) • **2.** to fail • **3.** to die.

    usage example (1):   [to fall]
                As I was riding my bike, I lost my balance and **bit the dust**.

    translation: As I was riding my bike, I lost my balance and fell.

    usage example (2):   [to fail]
                I think I really **bit the dust** on the final exam.

    translation: I think I really failed the final examination.

    NOTE: *"Exam"* is a popular abbreviation for *"examination."*

    usage example (3):   [to die]
                I just heard my old piano teacher **bit the dust**.

    translation: I just heard my old piano teacher died.

    NOTE: When this expression is used to mean "to die," its connotation is disrespectful and indifferent.

Ted "bit the dust" skiing down the hill.

blind leading the blind (the) *exp.* said of a situation where an inexperienced or incapable person is being instructed by someone equally inexperienced or incapable.

usage example (1): Jim is teaching Tom how to play tennis? That's a real case of **the blind leading the blind**.

translation: Jim is teaching Tom how to play tennis? That's a real case of an inexperienced person being taught by someone equally inexperienced.

usage example (2): My sister is the worst driver in the world. Now she wants to teach our brother how to drive. Talk about **the blind leading the blind**!

translation: My sister is the worst driver in the world. Now she wants to teach our brother how to drive. This is certainly an example of an inexperienced person teaching another inexperienced person!

NOTE: *"Talk about..."* is an extremely popular expression meaning "This is certainly an example of..."

brush with death (to have a) *exp.* to have a near-death experience.

usage example (1): I hear you almost got hit by a bus yesterday! You really had a **brush with death**.

translation: I hear you almost got hit by a bus yesterday! You really had a near-death experience.

usage example (2): As we drove around the corner, there was a huge truck driving toward us in our lane! I've never had such a close **brush with death** before!

translation: As we drove around the corner, there was a huge truck driving toward us in our lane! I've never had such a near-death experience before!

"Don't hold your breath" *exp.* "Don't anticipate that happening."

usage example (1): I know she said she'd remember to take you to the airport, but **don't hold your breath**. She forgets everything!

translation: I know she said she'd remember to take you to the airport, but don't anticipate that happening. She forgets everything!

usage example (2): I realize you want this promotion, but **don't hold your breath**. The owner's son is hoping for the same promotion as you.

translation: I realize you want this promotion, but don't anticipate that happening. The owner's son is hoping for the same promotion as you.

"Easy does it!" *exp.* • 1. "Be careful and go slowly!" • 2. "Calm down!"

usage example (1): ["Becareful and go slowly!"]
Let's lift this couch on the count of three. But **easy does it**! I know you have a weak back.

translation: Let's lift this couch on the count of three. But be careful! I know you have a weak back.

usage example (2): ["Calm down!"]
Easy does it! I don't like being yelled at like this.

translation: Calm down! I don't like being yelled at like this.

feet wet (to get one's) *exp.* to try a new experience for the first time.

usage example (1): I've never played golf before. I'm just **getting my feet wet**.

translation: I've never played golf before. I'm just experiencing it for the first time.

usage example (2): Would you like to join us for a game of bowling tonight? We're all just **getting our feet wet**.

translation: Would you like to join us for a game of bowling tonight? We're all trying it for the first time.

get the hang of something (to) *exp.* to learn how to do something.

usage example (1): When I first went skiing, I kept falling down. But after a few hours, I started **to get the hang of it**!

translation: When I first went skiing, I kept falling down. But after a few hours, I started to learn how to ski better!

usage example (2): I don't think I'll ever **get the hang** of playing the piano.

translation: I don't think I'll ever learn how to play the piano.

Bob's trying "to get the hang of" his new fax machine.

get up enough nerve to do something (to) *exp.* to summon the courage to do something.

usage example (1): I couldn't **get up enough nerve** to tell him he was fired.

translation: I couldn't summon enough courage to tell him he was fired.

usage example (2): Maybe if I have a drink, I'll be able **to get up enough nerve** to ask Tessa out on a date.

translation: Maybe if I have a drink, I'll be able to summon enough courage to ask Tessa out on a date.

VARIATION: **to get up the nerve to do something** *exp.*

hold one's own (to) *exp.* to be very capable at something (without any assistance).

usage example (1): Doug **holds his own** as an airplane pilot.

translation: Doug is very capable as an airplane pilot.

usage example (2): I can certainly **hold my own** on the dance floor.

translation: I'm very capable at dancing.

NOTE (1): The phrase *"when it comes to"* (meaning "with regard to") commonly follows this expression.

usage example: I can hold my own **when it comes to golf**.

translation: I am capable with regard to golf.

NOTE (2): The phrase *"in the [verb+ing] department"* may also follow this expression.

usage example: I can hold my own **in the golfing/ singing/cooking/etc. department**.

translation: I am very capable at golfing/singing/ cooking/etc.

second wind (to get one's) *exp.* to get a second burst of energy.

usage example (1): During the race, I started getting tired after about five minutes. Then all of a sudden, I got **my second wind** and won the race!

translation: During the race, I started getting tired after about five minutes. Then all of a sudden, I got a second burst of energy and won the race!

usage example (2): I just got my **second wind**. Let's go jogging again.

translation: I just got a second burst of energy. Let's go jogging again.

Practice The Vocabulary 📼

(Answers to Lesson 7, p. 265)

A. CROSSWORD
Fill in the crossword puzzle on the opposite page by choosing the correct word(s) from the list below.

bite the dust	feet wet
blind	hang
breath	nerve
brush	own
easy does it	second wind

Across

4. I'm scared to ski down the hill. I just know I'm going to _____ .

17. I don't think I could get up enough _____ to go ice skating. I'd be too scared I'd fall.

24. She's only been playing the guitar for two months but she can already hold her _____ .

32. I had a _____ with death when that truck almost hit me.

36. You're going to teach your sister to drive? But you know you're a terrible driver! This is certainly a case of the blind leading the _____ .

37. I've never been skating before. I'm just getting my _____ .

Down

4. You expect me to embarass myself by singing in front of an audience? Don't hold your _____ .

7. Take this glass of water to the table but _____ . It's filled all the way to the top.

9. Yesterday, I went waterskiing for the first time. I kept falling in the beginning. Then all of a sudden, I got the _____ of it and never fell again!

13. I just got my _____ . I think I'm ready to go jogging again.

CROSSWORD PUZZLE

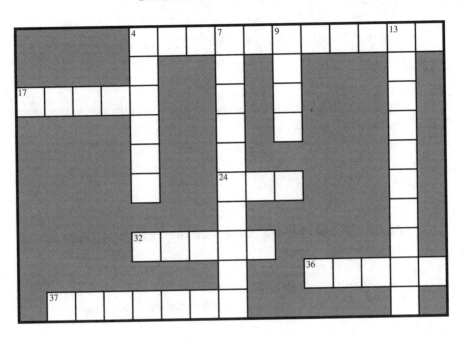

B. Choose the correct phrase that best fits the idiom.

1. **You really bit the dust going down that hill!**
   - ☐ a. Are you hurt?
   - ☐ b. I didn't know you could ski so well.
   - ☐ c. You went all the way down the hill without even falling.

2. **Easy does it!**
   - ☐ a. This isn't difficult at all.
   - ☐ b. If you're not careful, you could hurt yourself.
   - ☐ c. You don't have to be so careful.

3. **I'm getting my second wind.**
   - ☐ a. I'm really tired.
   - ☐ b. I'm having trouble breathing.
   - ☐ c. Let's go play some more tennis.

4. **Surfing was really difficult at first, but I'm finally getting the hang of it.**
   ☐ a. I'm a lot better than I was last week.
   ☐ b. I'm not as good as I was last week.
   ☐ c. I'll never be a good surfer.

5. **Being afraid of heights, I know I'd never get up the nerve to go sky-diving.**
   ☐ a. I'm not scared of it at all.
   ☐ b. I can't wait to go!
   ☐ c. I'd be too scared.

6. **Nancy and Dominic can really hold their own when it comes to ice skating.**
   ☐ a. They're terrible ice skaters.
   ☐ b. They're very good ice skaters.
   ☐ c. They're going ice skating today for the first time.

7. **You're not going to believe what happened to me today. I had a brush with death!**
   ☐ a. An enormous truck almost hit me as I was trying to walk across the street.
   ☐ b. I'm in perfect health.
   ☐ c. I have a slight cold.

8. **Here's a case of the blind leading the blind.**
   ☐ a. Peggy is going to teach Jim how to play the guitar. She's been playing guitar for many years.
   ☐ b. Peggy is going to teach Jim how to play the guitar. She had her first lesson only yesterday.
   ☐ c. Peggy and Jim are going to take guitar lessons together starting next week.

C. Complete the dialogue using the appropriate idioms from the list below.

bite the dust	**get my second wind**
easy does it	**getting your feet wet**
get the hang of	**hold your own**
get up enough nerve	**to have a brush with death**

Tim: I need to rest until I **(1)**_____.

I didn't know tennis was so tiring!

Bob: Don't worry about it. You're only **(2)**_____

_____ . You'll **(3)**_____ it

soon. Actually, you can already **(4)**_____ .

You played a great game today!

Tim: I hope I can **(5)**_____ to play with

my father next week. I just don't want to slip on the tennis court

and **(6)**_____ right in front of him.

Bob: You sound like you expect **(7)**_____

_____ right on the tennis court. As long as

you're not too aggressive when you hit the ball, you'll be fine.

Remember, **(8)**_____ .

D. CONTEXT EXERCISE
Choose the best idiom from the right column that goes with the phrase in the left column.

☐ 1. Are you going to invite Eric to your party?

☐ 2. Have you ice skated many times before?

☐ 3. How was your first day of skiing?

☐ 4. Would you like to play another game of tennis or are you too tired?

☐ 5. Do you really think I'll be able to learn how to play chess?

☐ 6. When we lift these boxes, be careful not to hurt your back.

☐ 7. Are you ready to give your presentation in front of the entire class?

☐ 8. I hear you're a very good singer.

☐ 9. Greg is teaching Steve about baseball? Greg doesn't know anything about baseball and Steve isn't athletic.

☐ 10. Are you all right? That truck came within inches of hitting you!

A. I can **hold my own**.

B. I had a great time even though I kept **biting the dust**.

C. No! I'm just **getting my feet wet**.

D. I'll be fine just as soon as I get my **second wind**.

E. I don't think I can **get up enough nerve**!

F. This is a definite case of **the blind leading the blind**.

G. I know. I really had a **brush with death**!

H. Of course. You'll **get the hang of it** in just a few hours.

I. I was going to give you the same advice. Remember, **easy does it**.

J. **Don't hold your breath**! I don't even like him.

E. DICTATION
Test Your Oral Comprehension
(This dictation can be found in Appendix A on page 278).

If you are following along with your cassette, you will now hear a paragraph containing many of the idioms from this section. The paragraph will be read by a native speaker at normal conversational speed (which may seem fast to you at first). In addition, the words will be pronounced *as you would actually hear them in a conversation,* including many common reductions.

The first time the paragraph is presented, simply listen in order to get accustomed to the speed and heavy use of reductions. The paragraph will then be read again with a pause after each group of words to give you time to write down what you heard. The third time the paragraph is read, follow along with what you have written.

Paul's "eyes are bigger than his stomach."

Lesson Eight - POPULAR IDIOMS

Dialogue In Slang

Paul's "eyes are bigger than his stomach"

DIALOGUE

At the restaurant.

Paul: I bet you had **to pull some strings** to get reservations at this restaurant. It's absolutely packed here!

Donna: The food is supposed to be **out of this world** and they don't **pad the bill** like the restaurant down the street. Look at this menu! Let's order three main dishes and split them. I **have a weakness** for fish.

Paul: I think **your eyes are bigger than your stomach**. Did you see how much food they give you? Look at that woman over there. I **can't make heads or tails out of** what she's eating but look at the size of that portion!

Donna: Good. I'm starving. By the way, if you **have a sweet tooth**, they're known for their incredible desserts. Gee, I hope our waiter **gets on the stick**. Why don't you try **to catch his eye**.

Paul: I haven't seen him since we sat down. I think he **vanished into thin air**.

Lesson Eight - POPULAR IDIOMS

Translation of dialogue  in standard English

DIALOGUE

At the restaurant.

Paul: I bet you had **to use your influence** to get reservations at this restaurant. It's absolutely packed here!

Donna: The food is supposed to be **extraordinary** and they don't **add extra charges to the bill** like the restaurant down the street. Look at this menu! Let's order three main dishes and split them. I **have a passion** for fish.

Paul: I think **you're anticipating being able to eat more than you can**. Did you see how much food they give you? Look at that woman over there. I **can't determine** what she's eating but look at the size of that portion!

Donna: Good. I'm starving. By the way, if you **love sweets**, they're known for their incredible desserts. Gee, I hope our waiter **gets more efficient and speedier**. Why don't you try **to get his attention**.

Paul: I haven't seen him since we sat down. I think he **completely disappeared.**

Dialogue in slang as it would be heard

Paul's "eyes 'r bigger then 'is stomach"

DIALOGUE

At the restaurant.

Paul: I betcha had **ta pull s'm strings** ta get reservations at this rest'rant. It's absolutely packed here!

Donna: The food's suppos' ta be **oudda this world** an' they don't **pad the bill** like the rest'rant down the street. Look 'it this menu! Let's order three main dishes n' splid 'em. I **have a weakness** fer fish.

Paul: I think **yer eyes 'r bigger th'n yer stomach**. Di 'ju see how much food they give you? Look 'it that woman over there. I **can't make heads 'r tails oud of** what she's eading but look 'it the size 'a that portion!

Donna: Good. I'm starving. By the way, if you **have a sweet tooth**, they're known fer their incredible desserts. Gee, I hope 'R waider **gets on the stick**. Why donchu try **da catch 'iz eye**.

Paul: I haven't seen 'im since we sat down. I think 'e **vanished inta thin air**.

Vocabulary

catch someone's eye (to) *exp.* to attract someone's attention.

    usage example (1): That painting really **caught my eye**.

        translation: That painting really attracted my attention.

    usage example (2): There's Tony. Try **to catch his eye**.

        translation: There's Tony. Try to get his attention.

eyes bigger than one's stomach (to have) *exp.* to anticipate being able to eat more food than one really can.

    usage example (1): Look at all that food you ordered! I think **your eyes are bigger than your stomach**.

        translation: Look at all that food you ordered! I think you anticipated being able to eat more food than you can.

    usage example (2): You think you could eat that entire cake? I think **your eyes are bigger than your stomach**.

        translation: You think you could eat that entire cake? I think your appetite is smaller than you realize.

get on the stick (to) *exp.* to become more efficient and speedier.

Lee S. Cargot is always late for work. He really needs "to get on the stick" or he may get fired!

usage example (1):   **Get on the stick**! We have to leave here in five minutes!

translation: Hurry! We have to leave here in five minutes!

usage example (2):   If Karen doesn't **get on the stick**, I'm leaving without her.

translation: If Karen doesn't hurry, I'm leaving without her.

have a sweet tooth (to) *exp.* to love sweets.

usage example (1):   I have a **sweet tooth**. I could eat candy for every meal!

translation: I love sweets. I could eat candy for every meal!

usage example (2):   I never developed a **sweet tooth**. I guess that's why I don't have any cavities.

translation: I never developed a love for sweets. I guess that's why I don't have any cavities.

Miss Pratt has a "sweet tooth."

have a weakness for something (to) *exp.* to have a passion for something.

usage example (1): I **have a weakness** for chocolate.

translation: I have a passion for chocolate!

usage example (2): I **have a weakness** for little babies.

translation: I love little babies.

SYNONYM: **to have a thing for something** *exp.*

usage example: I **have a thing** for the pastries they serve in this restaurant.

translation: I have a passion for the pastries they serve in this restaurant.

out of this world (to be) *exp.* to be extraordinary.

usage example (1): This dinner is **out of this world**.

translation: This dinner is extraordinary.

usage example (2): Her performance was **out of this world**.

translation: Her performance was extraordinary.

pad the bill (to) *exp.* to add extra charges to a bill.

usage example (1): How could this restaurant bill be so expensive? I wonder if the waiter **padded the bill**.

translation: How could this restaurant bill be so expensive? I wonder if the waiter added extra charges to the bill.

usage example (2): The hotel charged us for twenty telephone calls to Los Angeles that we didn't make. I think they're trying **to pad the bill**.

translation: The hotel charged us for twenty telephone calls to Los Angeles that we didn't make. I think they're trying to add extra charges to th bill.

pull some strings (to) *exp.* to use one's influence.

usage example (1):   I'll have **to pull some strings** to get a reservation at this restaurant with such short notice.

translation: I'll have to use my influence to get a reservation at this restaurant with such short notice.

usage example (2):   I had **to pull some strings** to get you hired, but I know it was worth it.

translation: I had to use my influence to get you hired, but I know it was worth it.

unable to make heads or tails [out] of someone or something (to be) *exp.* to be unable to make sense of someone or something.

usage example (1):   Sometimes Mark is so nice and other times he's so nasty. I just can't **make heads or tails [out] of** him.

translation: Sometimes Mark is so nice and other times he's so nasty. I just can't make sense of him.

usage example (2):   Did you see the painting he did? I can't **make heads or tails [out] of** it.

translation: Did you see the painting he did? I can't make sense of it.

vanish into thin air (to) *exp.* to disappear completely.

usage example (1):   I was speaking with an elderly woman and turned away for just a few seconds. When I turned back, she had **vanished into thin air**!

translation: I was speaking with an elderly woman and turned away for just a few seconds. When I turned back, she had completely disappeared!

usage example (2):   I can't find my wallet anywhere. It just **vanished into thin air**!

translation: I can't find my wallet anywhere. It just disappeared!

Practice the Vocabulary

(Answers to Lesson 8, p. 266)

A. Underline the word that best completes the phrase.

1. I love desserts. I have a real sweet (**foot, tooth, elbow**).

2. There's Irene! I don't think she sees us. See if you can catch her (**spleen, liver, eye**).

3. Last night, I went to the movies and saw the most beautiful love story. I guess I have a (**sickness, weakness, feebleness**) for romantic movies.

4. How are you going to eat all that? I think your eyes are bigger than your (**head, ears, stomach**).

5. I really had to (**push, pull, throw**) some strings to get reservations at this restaurant.

6. The movie was out of this (**world, planet, earth**)!

7. Where's Charlie? He vanished into (**thin, fat, obese**) air!

8. What's she holding? I can't make (**heads, feet, arms**) or tails [out] of it.

B. Complete the idioms by choosing the appropriate word from the list below.

air	**strings**
eye	**tails**
eyes	**tooth**
stick	**weakness**

1. I've never seen anyone eat as much chocolate as you. You must really have a sweet _____ .

2. You could eat that entire cake? I think your _____ are bigger than your stomach.

3. The burglar vanished into thin _____ .

4. I know you have a _____ for pies, so I baked you an apple pie for dessert.

5. I really had to pull some _____ to get this present delivered to you in time for your birthday.

6. Did you see the dessert Joan made? What was it? I couldn't make heads or _____ [out] of it.

7. You'd better get on the _____ . We're already late.

8. That painting really caught my _____ . Is it an original?

C. CONTEXT EXERCISE
Choose the idiom from the right column that best defines the word(s) in italics from the left column.

☐ 1. I can't *determine* what the problem is with your car.

A. **vanished into thin air**

☐ 2. There's our waitress. Try to *get her attention.*

B. **pull some strings**

C. **catch her eye**

☐ 3. I have a *passion* for French food.

☐ 4. You really need to get *more efficient and speedier!*

D. **your eyes are bigger than your stomach**

☐ 5. I think *you anticipate being able to eat more than you actually can.*

E. **have a sweet tooth**

F. **on the stick**

☐ 6. I *love sweets.*

G. **weakness**

☐ 7. He *totally disappeared!*

☐ 8. I had to *use my influence* to get tickets to this play.

H. **make heads or tails [out] of**

D. WORD SEARCH
Circle the words in the grid on the opposite page that complete the following idiomatic expressions. Words may be spelled up, down, or diagonally. The first one has been done for you.

1. **have a _____ for something (to)** *exp.* to have a passion for something.

2. **_____ some strings to get something (to)** *exp.* to use one's influence to get something.

3. **out of this _____ (to be)** *exp.* to be extraordinary.

4. **_____ the bill (to)** *exp.* to add extra charges to a bill.

5. **eyes bigger than one's _____ (to have)** *exp.* to anticipate being able to eat more than one actually can.

6. **unable to make _____ or tails [out] of someone or something (to be)** *exp.* to be unable to evaluate someone or something.

7. **have a sweet _____ (to)** *exp.* to love sweets.

8. **get on the _____ (to)** *exp.* to get more efficient and speedier.

9. **_____ someone's eye (to)** *exp.* to attract someone's attention.

10. **vanish into _____ air (to)** *exp.* to disappear completely.

WORD SEARCH

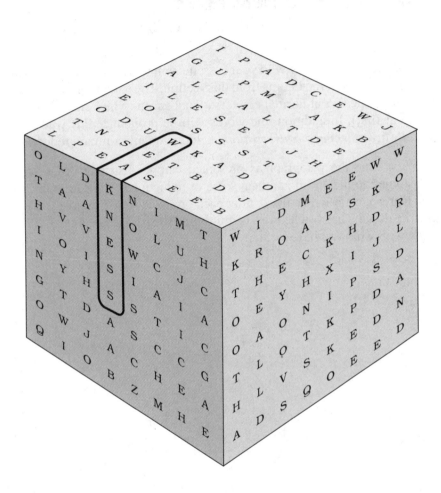

E. DICTATION
Test Your Oral Comprehension
(This dictation can be found in Appendix A on page 279).

If you are following along with your cassette, you will now hear a paragraph containing many of the idioms from this section. The paragraph will be read by a native speaker at normal conversational speed (which may seem fast to you at first). In addition, the words will be pronounced *as you would actually hear them in a conversation,* including many common reductions.

The first time the paragraph is presented, simply listen in order to get accustomed to the speed and heavy use of reductions. The paragraph will then be read again with a pause after each group of words to give you time to write down what you heard. The third time the paragraph is read, follow along with what you have written.

Lesson Nine - POPULAR IDIOMS

Dialogue In Slang

I'm not going to "take this lying down"

DIALOGUE

Dave and Eric's plans are ruined.

Dave: I guess we can't go to the movies tonight. My younger brother borrowed my car again without asking. **Come to think of it**, this is the third time this month he's done that!

Eric: I'd **nip that in the bud** if I were **in your shoes**.

Dave: Well, if he thinks I'm going to **take this lying down**, he's got **another think coming**! This time I'm going to **let him have it**! He's got to learn to respect my things.

Eric: If he's anything like my brother, don't bother trying to get him to **turn over a new leaf**. You're just **beating your head against the wall**. There's only one thing you can do. **Take it in stride**.

Dave: Well, when he wants to borrow my car next time, I'll tell him that it's **out of the question**.

Lesson Nine - POPULAR IDIOMS

Translation of dialogue 〈in standard English

DIALOGUE

Dave and Eric's plans are ruined.

Dave: I guess we can't go to the movies tonight. My younger brother borrowed my car again without asking. **In thinking about it more**, this is the third time this month he's done that!

Eric: I'd **put a stop to that quickly** if I were **in your situation**.

Dave: Well, if he thinks I'm going to **be passive about this**, he's **destined for an unpleasant surprise**! This time I'm going to **reprimand him**! He's got to learn to respect my things.

Eric: If he's anything like my brother, don't bother trying to get him to **change his bad habits**. It's **useless**. There's only one thing you can do. **Accept it calmly**.

Dave: Well, when he wants to borrow my car next time, I'll tell him that it's **not even going to be considered.**

Lesson Nine - POPULAR IDIOMS

Dialogue in slang as it would be heard

I'm not gonna "take this lying down"

DIALOGUE

Dave and Eric's plans 'r ruined.

Dave: I guess we can't go da the movies t'night. My younger brother borrowed my car again withoud asking. **Come ta think of it**, this is the third time this month he's done that!

Eric: I'd **nip thad 'n the bud** if I were **in yer shoes**.

Dave: Well, if he thinks I'm gonna **take this lying down**, he's god **another think coming**! This time I'm gonna **let 'im have it**! He's godda learn ta respect my things.

Eric: If e's anything like my brother, don't bother trying ta ged 'im ta **turn over a new leaf**. Y'r jus' **beading yer head against the wall**. There's only one thing you c'n do. **Take id 'n stride**.

Dave: Well, when 'e wants ta borrow my car nex' time, I'll tell 'im thad it's **oudda the question**.

Vocabulary

another think coming (to have) *exp.* to be destined for an unpleasant surprise.

> *usage example (1):* If you really believe you're not going to get caught for cheating on the test, you've **got another think coming**.

> *translation:* If you really believe you're not going to get caught for cheating on the test, you're destined for an unpleasant surprise.

> *usage example (2):* If Peter thinks he can just come in here and take my equipment without asking, he's **got another think coming**.

> *translation:* If Peter thinks he can just come in here and take my equipment without asking, he's going to get an unpleasant surprise.

> **NOTE:** A common misconception even among native speakers of English is that this expression is *"to have another thing coming."* The reason for this is because the letter *"k"* in *"think"* and the *"c"* in *"coming"* share the same sound. Therefore, when pronounced together quickly, *"thing coming"* and *"think coming"* have the same sound.

beat one's head against the wall (to) *exp.* to waste one's time trying to achieve something.

> *usage example (1):* If you're going to try and get our professor to change your grade, you're **beating your head against the wall**.

> *translation:* If you're going to try and get our professor to change your grade, you're wasting your time.

> *usage example (2):* You're going to try to teach Ed how to use a computer? Believe me, you're **beating your head against the wall**.

translation: You're going to try to teach Ed how to use a computer? Believe me, you're wasting your time.

"Come to think of it..." *exp.* "In thinking about it more..."

usage example (1): I wonder if it was John who stole your wallet. **Come to think of it**, I did see him with a wallet that looked just like yours!

translation: I wonder if it was John who stole your wallet. In thinking about it more, I did see him with a wallet that looked just like yours!

usage example (2): Would you like to go to Hawaii on vacation this summer? **Come to think of it**, that's where Jim and Megan are going, too. Maybe we could all go together.

translation: Would you like to go to Hawaii on vacation this summer? In thinking about it more, that's where Jim and Megan are going, too. Maybe we could all go together.

in someone's shoes (to be) *exp.* to be in someone else's situation.

usage example (1): Your rent is due in two weeks! If I were **in your shoes**, I'd be looking for a job today instead of going to the movies.

translation: Your rent is due in two weeks! If I were in your situation, I'd be looking for a job today instead of going to the movies.

usage example (2): Grant's house burned down and he lost his job all in the same day. I sure wouldn't want to be **in his shoes**.

translation: Grant's house burned down and he lost his job all in the same day. I sure wouldn't want to be in his situation.

let someone have it (to) *exp.* to reprimand someone strongly.

    usage example (1): If he insults me again, I'm going **to let him have it**!

    translation: If he insults me again, I'm going to reprimand him.

    usage example (2): You should have seen the way Maggie **let John have it**!

    translation: You should have seen the way Maggie yelled at John!

SYNONYM: **to give it to someone** *exp.*

    usage example: My mother **gave it** to my brother for using her car without permission.

    translation: My mother reprimanded my brother for using her car without permission.

The boss looks like he's about
"to let someone have it!"

nip something in the bud (to) *exp.* to put a stop to something quickly before it has a chance to get worse (as one would stop the growth of a flower by clipping or "nipping" the bud).

> *usage example (1):*   The children were starting to fight over the ball so I **nipped it in the bud** by taking it away.
>
> *translation:*   The children were starting to fight over the ball so I put a stop to it quickly by taking it away.

> *usage example (2):*   Angie is starting an argument with a customer! I'm going **to nip that in the bud** right now.
>
> *translation:*   Angie is starting an argument with a customer! I'm going to put a stop to that right now.

take something in stride (to) *exp.* to accept something without getting upset.

> *usage example (1):*   She didn't seem too upset when her house burned down. She certainly **took it in stride**.
>
> *translation:*   She didn't seem too upset when her house burned down. She certainly accepted it without getting upset.

> *usage example (2):*   If you don't get the first job you apply for, just **take it in stride** and keep on trying.
>
> *translation:*   If you don't get the first job you apply for, just accept it without getting upset and keep on trying.

SYNONYM: **to let it slide** *exp.*

> *usage example:*   Don't get so angry! Just **let it slide**.
>
> *translation:*   Don't get so angry! Just accept it without getting upset!

take something lying down (to) *exp.* to accept something passively.

> *usage example (1):*   He just insulted you. Are you going **to take that lying down**?

translation: He just insulted you. Are you going to accept that passively?

usage example (2): He lied to me about where he was last night. I'm not going **to take that lying down**.

translation: He lied to me about where he was last night. I'm not going to accept that passively.

"That's out of the question!" *exp.* "There is absolutely no way that will be considered!"

usage example (1): You want to borrow my car to haul fertilizer? That's **out of the question**!

translation: You want to borrow my car to haul fertilizer? There's absolutely no way I'd consider that!

usage example (2): Your sister wants to stay with us for three months? That's **out of the question**!

translation: Your sister wants to stay with us for three months? There's absolutely no way I'd consider that!

turn over a new leaf (to) *exp.* to change one's bad habits.

usage example (1): As usual, I overate and now I feel sick. Starting tomorrow, I'm **turning over a new leaf**.

translation: As usual, I overate and now I feel sick. Starting tomorrow, I'm giving up my bad habits.

usage example (2): I'm never going to be late again. Starting right now, I'm **turning over a new leaf**.

translation: I'm never going to be late again. Starting right now, I'm changing my bad habits.

Practice The Vocabulary

(Answers to Lesson 9, p. 267)

A. CROSSWORD

Fill in the crossword puzzle on the opposite page by choosing the correct word(s) from the list below.

a new leaf	lying down
beating your head	nip that in the bud
come to think of it	question
have it	shoes
in stride	think

Across

16. She's never going to forgive you. You're just _____ against the wall.

19. Chris didn't seem upset about the fire. He just took it _____ .

23. I just bought an expensive car and now it's not working. I'm certainly not going to take this _____ . I'm going to get my money back!

31. Keith and Gordon are starting to fight again? I'm going to _____ right now!

34. If he thinks he can just borrow my car without asking, he has another _____ coming.

38. I've decided to turn over _____ . I'm going to exercise everyday.

44. I asked my mother if I could borrow $100, but she said it was out of the _____ . Maybe I should ask my father instead.

Down

9. _____ *exp.* "In thinking about it more."

14. I can't believe Ed told everyone my secret. I'm going to let him _____ !

29. Mark just lost his job and wrecked his car in the same day. I sure wouldn't want to be in his _____ .

CROSSWORD PUZZLE

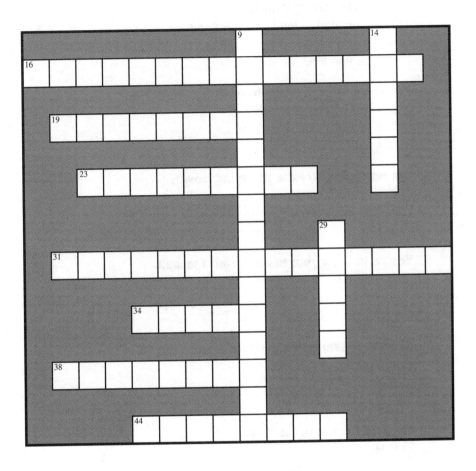

B. Choose the correct phrase that best fits the idiom.

1. That's **out of the question**.
   - ☐ a. I'd be glad to lend you some money.
   - ☐ b. I'd never lend you any money.
   - ☐ c. Can you lend me some money?

2. **I'm going to let Gordon have it!**
   - ☐ a. I'm really angry with him.
   - ☐ b. I'm really happy with him.
   - ☐ c. I really like him.

3. **I'm not going to take this lying down.**
   - ☐ a. I'm going to take a nap.
   - ☐ b. I'm going to go exercise.
   - ☐ c. I'm going to take action.

4. **You're beating your head against the wall.**
   - ☐ a. You'll be able to convince your father to lend you his car.
   - ☐ b. You'll never be able to convince your father to lend you his car.
   - ☐ c. You killed that poor animal.

5. **Nick takes everything in stride.**
   - ☐ a. Nothing upsets him.
   - ☐ b. Everything upsets him.
   - ☐ c. He looks very angry.

6. **I'm glad I'm not in his shoes.**
   - ☐ a. He's rich.
   - ☐ b. He has a wonderful life.
   - ☐ c. He has a terrible life.

7. **I'm going to nip that in the bud right now.**
   - ☐ a. I hope he continues to play his radio loudly.
   - ☐ b. I hope he plays his music all night.
   - ☐ c. I'm not going to let him play his loud music all night.

8. **I've decided to turn over a new leaf.**
   - ☐ a. I'm going to quit smoking, start eating right, and get exercise.
   - ☐ b. I'm never going to change.
   - ☐ c. I'm going to do some yard work.

C. Complete the dialogue using the appropriate idioms from the list below.

beating my head
come to think of it
got another think coming
in the bud

in your shoes
let him have it
out of the question
take this lying down

Sally: I'm not going to **(1)**_____! If my

little brother thinks he can use my telephone without asking, he's

(2)_____ . This time,

I'm going to **(3)**_____!

Grace: You really need to nip it **(4)**_____ before

he starts doing it every day. **(5)**_____ ,

isn't this the third time he's borrowed your telephone without

asking?

Sally: You're right. The next time he wants to use it, I'm going to tell

him that it's **(6)**_____ . I get

so frustrated sometimes. I'm **(7)**_____

against the wall, trying to get him to understand why I'm angry.

Grace: It must be so annoying living with a little brother. I'm glad I'm

not **(8)**_____ .

D. CONTEXT EXERCISE
Choose the best idiom from the right column that goes with the phrase in the left column.

☐ 1. Let's get some ice cream.

☐ 2. You'll never get him to admit he made a mistake.

☐ 3. Your neighbors are getting ready to burn a huge pile of garbage.

☐ 4. I never get upset about anything.

☐ 5. Would you buy me that necklace?

☐ 6. My father is going to kill me when he finds out that I broke his new hammer.

☐ 7. You have such a terrible temper.

☐ 8. I'm really angry with him.

A. You're right. I'm just **beating my head against the wall**.

B. I don't blame you! I think you should **let him have it**!

C. I noticed that. You **take everything in stride**.

D. Thanks for telling me. I'm going **to nip that in the bud** right now!

E. You're right. Starting today, I'll never get angry again. I'm **turning over a new leaf**.

F. I'm sure glad I'm **not in your shoes**.

G. That's **out of the question**. It's too expensive.

H. That sounds great! **Come to think of it**, I had ice cream yesterday. Let's get some candy instead.

E. DICTATION

Test Your Oral Comprehension

(This dictation can be found in Appendix A on page 279).

If you are following along with your cassette, you will now hear a paragraph containing many of the idioms from this section. The paragraph will be read by a native speaker at normal conversational speed (which may seem fast to you at first). In addition, the words will be pronounced *as you would actually hear them in a conversation,* including many common reductions.

The first time the paragraph is presented, simply listen in order to get accustomed to the speed and heavy use of reductions. The paragraph will then be read again with a pause after each group of words to give you time to write down what you heard. The third time the paragraph is read, follow along with what you have written.

Sally is "showing her true colors!"

Lesson Ten - POPULAR IDIOMS

Sally is "showing her true colors"

DIALOGUE

Sally's in trouble!

Cecily: You're not going to believe what happened today. You've got to promise to **keep it to yourself**.

Carol: Sure, **what gives**?

Cecily: Today Mr. Peters threw Sally Gibbons out of class!

Carol: **On the level**?

Cecily: **I'll say**. I knew Sally would finally **show her true colors**. When she got her final test results back from Mr. Peters, she **went off on him**. You should have heard her. I've never seen anyone get so **worked up** before. **To make a long story short**, it seems that Mr. Peters failed her because he caught her cheating.

Carol: That's **no laughing matter**. That means she'll have to take the whole course again. I can't believe she's going to have **to start from square one**.

Cecily: **It serves her right**!

Lesson Ten - POPULAR IDIOMS

Translation of dialogue  in standard English

DIALOGUE

Sally's in trouble!

Cecily: You're not going to believe what happened today. You've got to promise to **keep it a secret**.

Carol: Sure, **what's been happening**?

Cecily: Today Mr. Peters threw Sally Gibbons out of class!

Carol: **Really**?

Cecily: **Absolutely**. I knew Sally would finally **reveal her true personality**. When she got her final test results back from Mr. Peters, she **started yelling at him**. You should have heard her. I've never seen anyone get so **upset** before. **In summary**, it seems that Mr. Peters failed her because he caught her cheating.

Carol: That's **serious**. That means she'll have to take the whole course again. I can't believe she's going to have **to start from the beginning**.

Cecily: **That's just what she deserves**!

Lesson Ten - POPULAR IDIOMS

Dialogue in slang as it would be heard

Sally is "showing her true colors"

DIALOGUE

Sally's in trouble!

Cecily: Y're not gonna b'lieve what happened t'day. You've godda promise ta **keep it ta yerself**.

Carol: Sh'r, **what gives**?

Cecily: T'day Mr. Peders threw Sally Gibbons oud of class!

Carol: **On the level**?

Cecily: **All say**. I knew Sally would fin'lly **show 'er true colors**. When she got 'er final test results back fr'm Mr. Peders, she **wen' off on 'im**. You should've heard 'er. I've never seen anyone get so **worked up** b'fore. **Ta make a long story short**, it seems that Mr. Peders failed 'er b'cause 'e caught 'er cheading.

Carol: That's **no laughing madder**. That means she'll haf ta take the whole course again. I can't b'lieve she's gonna haf **ta start from square one**.

Cecily: **It serves 'er right!**

Vocabulary

get [all] worked up about something (to) *exp.* to become very upset about something.

    usage example (1): Just because Nancy spilled the milk, you don't have **to get [all] worked up about it**. I'll have it cleaned up in a minute!

    translation: Just because Nancy spilled the milk, you don't have to get so upset about it. I'll have it cleaned up in a minute!

    usage example (2): My mother **got [all] worked up** because I forgot to buy bread at the market.

    translation: My mother got upset because I forgot to buy bread at the market.

    VARIATION: **to get [all] worked up over something** *exp.*

Pete and Ed are getting "[all] worked up!"

go off on someone (to) *exp.* to yell angrily at someone.

usage example (1):   If he says anything about my weight, I'm going **to go off on him**.

translation: If he says anything about my weight, I'm going to yell at him.

usage example (2):   My sister **went off on me** because I forgot to tell her that her boyfriend called.

translation: My sister yelled at me because I forgot to tell her that her boyfriend called.

I'll say! *exp.* • 1. "Absolutely!" • 2. "You're absolutely right!"

usage example (1):   "Do you think he's handsome?" **"I'll say!"**

translation: "Do you think he's handsome?" "Absolutely!"

usage example (2):   "It's raining so hard today!" **"I'll say!"**

translation: "It's raining so hard today!" "You're absolutely right!"

NOTE: When pronouncing this expression, it's important to put the emphasis on *"I'll"* giving it a higher pitch than *"say."*

keep something to oneself (to) *exp.* to keep something secret.

usage example (1):   You have **to keep this to yourself**. I just found out that Maggie won the election but it won't be announced until tomorrow.

translation: You have to keep this secret. I just found out that Maggie won the election but it won't be announced until tomorrow.

usage example (2):   If you're going to say something mean about her, just **keep it to yourself**.

translation: If you're going to say something mean about her, just keep it secret.

no laughing matter (to be) *exp.* said of a serious situation.

usage example (1): This is **no laughing matter**. If you don't pass this test, you're not going to graduate.

translation: This is a serious situation. If you don't pass this test, you're not going to graduate.

usage example (2): It's **no laughing matter**. You could get arrested for what you did.

translation: It's not funny. You could get arrested for what you did.

on the level (to be) *exp.* to be telling the truth.

usage example (1): The salesman said he's giving us the best price in town. Do you think he's **on the level**?

translation: The salesman said he's giving us the best price in town. Do you think he's being truthful?

usage example (2): "Susie and Ron got married yesterday!" "**On the level**?"

translation: "Susan and Ron got married yesterday!" "Truthfully?"

serve someone right (to) *exp.* to suffer the consequences that one deserves.

usage example (1): The school isn't going to let Jennifer graduate because she was caught cheating on her final exam. It **serves her right**!

translation: The school isn't going to let Jennifer graduate because she was caught cheating on her final exam. She's getting what she deserves!

usage example (2):   Ben lied about his experience when he applied for this job and today the boss gave him an assignment that he's not qualified to do. If he doesn't get it done, the boss will fire him. I guess it **serves him right** for lying.

translation: Ben lied about his experience when he applied for this job and today the boss gave him an assignment that he's not qualified to do. If he doesn't get it done, the boss will fire him. I guess he's going to get what he deserves as a consequence for lying.

show one's true colors (to)   *exp.* to reveal one's true personality.

usage example (1):   We all thought Cathy was a timid person but when she saved a child from a burning building, she **showed her true colors**.

translation: We all thought Cathy was a timid person but when she saved a child from a burning building, she showed her true personality.

usage example (2):   My best friend has been telling lies about me. I always thought he was so loyal, but I guess I was wrong. He's finally **showing his true colors**.

translation: My best friend has been telling lies about me. I always thought he was so loyal, but I guess I was wrong. He's finally revealing the kind of person he really is.

start from square one (to)   *exp.* to start from the very beginning.

usage example (1):   There are some parts of your story that I don't understand. **Start from square one**.

translation: There are some parts of your story that I don't understand. Start from the beginning.

usage example (2):   I was typing my book on the computer when suddenly the electricity went off and I lost everything. I had **to start from square one**.

> *translation:* I was typing my book on the computer when suddenly the electricity went off and I lost everything. I had to start again from the very beginning.

"To make a long story short..." *exp.* "In summary..."

usage example (1): **To make a long story short**, Jeff is taking me to France next month!

translation: In summary, Jeff is taking me to France next month!

usage example (2): First I missed the bus, then I didn't have any money to call a taxi. **To make a long story short**, Stephanie came to my rescue.

translation: First I missed the bus, then I didn't have any money to call a taxi. In summary, Stephanie came to my rescue.

"What gives?" *exp.* "What's happening?"

usage example (1): You all look so sad. **What gives**?

translation: You all look so sad. What's happening?

usage example (2): Yesterday, you were so nice to me and now you seem so angry. **What gives**?

translation: Yesterday, you were so nice to me and now you seem so angry. What's happening?

Practice the Vocabulary 📼

(Answers to Lesson 10, p. 268)

A. Were the following idioms used correctly or incorrectly?

1. Why are you getting **so worked up**? It's not such a big problem!
   ☐ correct   ☐ incorrect

2. It's **no laughing matter**. If we lose this client, our company will have to close forever.
   ☐ correct   ☐ incorrect

3. Irene is twelve years old. It **serves her right**!
   ☐ correct   ☐ incorrect

4. Betty is finally **showing her true colors**. Her hair is actually red.
   ☐ correct   ☐ incorrect

5. Your mother really **went off on you** this morning. Do you always fight like that?
   ☐ correct   ☐ incorrect

6. Make sure you **keep this information to yourself**. I want you to tell everyone.
   ☐ correct   ☐ incorrect

7. I can't believe I burned this cake. It took me four hours to make this. Now I have **to start from square one**.
   ☐ correct   ☐ incorrect

8. "Do you think Julie's pretty?" "**I'll say**! She's ugly!"
   ☐ correct   ☐ incorrect

B. Underline the appropriate word that best completes the phrase.

1. What (**gives, takes, receives**)? Did something bad happen to you today?

2. To make a long story (**long, longer, short**), I'm moving to Paris next week.

3. Peggy cheated on her test? On the (**slant, elevation, level**)?

4. Why are you getting so worked (**up, down, out**)? It's nothing to get upset about.

5. Did you see how mean Jack was yesterday? I knew he'd show his true (**colors, numbers, clothing**) one of these days.

6. The boss really went (**off, on, up**) on me for being late this morning.

7. John got fired for stealing money from the company. Frankly, it serves him (**straight, left, right**).

8. It took me three weeks to finish this painting. Today I ripped the canvas by accident. Now I have to start from (**circle, triangle, square**) one.

C. Choose the most appropriate definition of the words in boldface.

☐ 1. Why are you getting so **worked up**?
  ☐ a. upset and angry
  ☐ b. tired
  ☐ c. excited and happy

☐ 2. Is Jim being **on the level**?
  ☐ a. untruthful
  ☐ b. truthful
  ☐ c. stubborn

☐ 3. Your girlfriend really **went off on you**.
  ☐ a. yelled at you
  ☐ b. ran away from you
  ☐ c. hit you

☐ 4. **It serves you right** for lying!
  ☐ a. I'm mad at you
  ☐ b. I commend you
  ☐ c. You got the consequences you deserved

☐ 5. This is a secret, so you have to **keep it to yourself**.
  ☐ a. tell everyone
  ☐ b. listen carefully
  ☐ c. keep it a secret

☐ 6. Today Eric **showed his true colors**.
  ☐ a. showed us his colorful new shirt
  ☐ b. revealed his deepest secrets
  ☐ c. revealed his true personality

☐ 7. This is **no laughing matter**.
  ☐ a. extremely funny
  ☐ b. very serious
  ☐ c. mildly funny

☐ 8. **What gives**?
  ☐ a. What's happening
  ☐ b. Who gave you that
  ☐ c. What are you eating

D. CONTEXT EXERCISE
Choose the correct idiom that goes with the phrase.

1. You have to promise not to tell anyone this secret.
   - ☐ a. **I'll keep it to myself.**
   - ☐ b. **I'm on the level.**

2. Mitch got in trouble for stealing. Now he'll have to be in jail for a year.
   - ☐ a. **Now he'll have to start from square one.**
   - ☐ b. **Frankly, it serves him right.**

3. Jennifer's doctor just discovered she has a terrible infection.
   - ☐ a. **That's no laughing matter.**
   - ☐ b. **Now she'll have to start from square one.**

4. I'm angry about what Jay did to me. I supposed I should calm down.
   - ☐ a. **It serves you right!**
   - ☐ b. **It's nothing to get [all] worked up about.**

5. I just got fired today!
   - ☐ a. **On the level?**
   - ☐ b. **I'll say.**

6. Do you think David is handsome?
   - ☐ a. **It serves him right.**
   - ☐ b. **I'll say.**

7. I lost my briefcase which contained my entire report!
   - ☐ a. **Now I'll have to start from square one.**
   - ☐ b. **Now you're showing your true colors.**

8. Beverly started yelling at everyone for no reason.
   - ☐ a. **I knew she'd show her true colors.**
   - ☐ b. **Now she'll have to start from square one.**

E. DICTATION 📼
Test Your Oral Comprehension
(This dictation can be found in Appendix A on page 280).

If you are following along with your cassette, you will now hear a paragraph containing many of the idioms from this section. The paragraph will be read by a native speaker at normal conversational speed (which may seem fast to you at first). In addition, the words will be pronounced *as you would actually hear them in a conversation,* including many common reductions.

The first time the paragraph is presented, simply listen in order to get accustomed to the speed and heavy use of reductions. The paragraph will then be read again with a pause after each group of words to give you time to write down what you heard. The third time the paragraph is read, follow along with what you have written.

REVIEW EXAM
FOR LESSONS 6-10

(Answers to Review, p. 269)

A. Underline the appropriate word that best completes the phrase.

1. You really went to (**city, town, country**) on this party!

2. For the past two weeks, I've been trying to teach my mother how to drive. I don't think she'll ever get the (**hang, bang, gang**) of it.

3. Did you hear the (**split, hole, crack**) Gina made about Kevin? I always thought they were friends!

4. You want to go running again? I haven't gotten my second (**wind, breeze, gust**) yet.

5. What a beautiful restaurant! You must have had to pull some (**ropes, cords, strings**) to get reservations.

6. You'd better get on the (**branch, stick, wood**) or you'll be late.

7. You have nine children? I'm glad I'm not in your (**shoes, thongs, sandals**). I don't think I could do it!

8. I've been trying to explain the problem to him, but he'll just never understand it! I'm tired of beating my (**head, foot, elbow**) against the wall.

9. I made the most beautiful cake but I accidentally dropped it on the floor. Now I have to start from square (**one, two, three**) and make a new dessert.

10. Barbara got so mad that she started throwing things all over the office. I couldn't believe it. I thought she was such a calm person. Well, you always said she'd show her true (**colors, numbers, figures**) one of these days.

B. CROSSWORD

Step 1: Fill in the blanks with the appropriate word(s) from the list below.
Step 2: Using your answers, fill in the crossword puzzle on page 165.

a new leaf	dust	level
air	eye	nerve
blind	feet	stomach
breath	fishing	tails
brush	hair	tooth
case	in the bud	worked
dolled	laughing	world

Across

1. I'm going to turn over _____ . Starting today, I'm not going to eat so many candies.

6. Do you really think you can eat all of that? I think your eyes are bigger than your _____ .

7. I'm tired of you two fighting all the time. I'm going to nip this argument _____ right now!

11. Janice is teaching Barbara how to cook? That sure is a case of the blind leading the _____ . They're both terrible cooks.

12. I was riding my bicycle down the hill and I bit the _____ . I even tore my new pants.

Across *(continued)*

14. I can't go to the party tonight. I look terrible. I'm having a bad
_____ day.

17. This is my first time playing tennis. I'm just getting my
_____ wet.

18. Why are you getting all _____ up. Calm
down!

20. The chocolate cake Nancy made was out of this _____ !
I don't know when I've eaten anything so delicious.

Down

2. I don't think I could ever get up enough _____ to
go parachuting.

3. John stole ten dollars from the company. It's no _____
matter. He may go to jail.

4. Did you see the way Alice was waving her hand around so
everyone could see her engagement ring? You just know she's
_____ for a compliment.

5. My mother got on my _____ because I forgot my
sister's birthday. I'm going to get her a present right now.

Down (continued)

8. Did you see that painting Keith did? What's it supposed to be? I can't make heads or _____ out of it.

9. Carol said she would be here at seven o'clock, but don't hold your _____ . She's always late.

10. All the other girls at the high school reunion were all _____ up except for me!

11. The surgeon said that I had a _____ with death during the operation. I'm lucky to be alive!

13. You're always thinking about chocolate. I've never known anyone with such a sweet _____ .

15. Where's Wally? He was standing next to me just a moment ago. I know he couldn't have just vanished into thin _____ !

16. Steve just told me that the boss is going to close the company. I didn't believe him in the beginning, but he promised me that he was on the _____ .

19. What a beautiful necklace you're wearing. It caught my _____ the moment I entered the room.

CROSSWORD PUZZLE

C. TRUE or FALSE
Are the following sentences (containing idiomatic expressions) true or false?

1. If you're **all dolled up**, you're dressed badly.
   ☐ True   ☐ False

2. If your mother **gets on your case**, she's criticizing you.
   ☐ True   ☐ False

3. If you're **getting your feet wet** in an activity, you're very experienced.
   ☐ True   ☐ False

4. If someone says that the food is **out of this world**, it means that the food was imported.
   ☐ True   ☐ False

5. If you **have a sweet tooth**, you love sweets.
   ☐ True   ☐ False

6. If the restaurant **pads your bill**, you've been undercharged.
   ☐ True   ☐ False

7. If you **take something lying down**, you're actively trying to change something.
   ☐ True   ☐ False

8. If you **let someone have it**, you are reprimanding him/her.
   ☐ True   ☐ False

9. If you **keep something to yourself**, you are informing everyone.
   ☐ True   ☐ False

10. If you **turn over a new leaf**, you are changing your bad habits.
    ☐ True   ☐ False

D. CONTEXT EXERCISE
Choose the best idiom from the right column that goes with the phrase in the left column.

☐ 1. I'm not being allowed to graduate college because I failed the math final!

☐ 2. Greg got a speeding ticket.

☐ 3. Is your house guest still bothering you?

☐ 4. May I borrow your sweater tonight?

☐ 5. I wonder who took my wallet.

☐ 6. I wish I didn't get so upset about little problems.

☐ 7. Did you see the new employee? He's so handsome!

☐ 8. What's he eating?

☐ 9. I wonder if my parents will buy me a new car for graduation.

☐ 10. I lent George ten dollars because he said he needed money for the bus.

A. That's **out of the question**. Every time you use something of mine, you ruin it.

B. I see you still **have a weakness** for tall blonds.

C. **On the level**? Won't they let you take the test again?

D. I don't know. **Come to think of it**, Peter was the only person in your house last night. Maybe he took it by accident!

E. **It serves him right**. He needs to learn to drive slower.

F. **Don't hold your breath**. Do you know how expensive that would be?

G. I can't believe you **bought into** that! He's a millionaire!

H. I don't know. **I can't make heads or tails out of it**.

I. **I'll say**. I don't think he'll ever leave!

J. Maybe you need to learn how **to take things in stride**.

SPECIALTY IDIOMS & PHRASES

✔ **Two-, Three-, and Four-Syllable Idioms Beginning with the Same Letter**

    knick-knack • mish-mash • criss-cross

✔ **Repeating Words**

    so-so • bye-bye • up-and-up

✔ **Proverbs**

    The shoe's on the other foot
    Out of sight, out of mind
    Actions speak louder than words

✔ **Survival Words & Phrases (That Could Save Your Life!)**

    Freeze! • Hand it over! • Step outta the car!

Lesson Eleven - ALLITERATION

Dialogue In Slang

Earl finds an interesting "knick-knack"

DIALOGUE

A day of housecleaning.

Earl: Did you see this **knick knack** I found?

Anne: Where did you get that?

Earl: In this box of **bric-a-brac** your mother's been saving. What a **mish mash** of junk. For a person who likes everything **spic-and-span**, she sure did let everything get dirty.

Anne: Look! Here's my old **ping-pong** paddle! And my grandfather's watch! I haven't seen that in years. I always liked the **criss-cross** pattern on the back. Listen. It still works! Hear it going **tick-tock**? It's still in **tip-top** shape. I'm so excited that my grandparents are coming here next week. I know they're going to love their new grandchild.

Earl: I just hope they have the energy to play with him.

Anne: Oh, they're both full of **vim-and-vigor**. They absolutely love the **pitter-patter** of little feet around the house, too.

Lesson Eleven - ALLITERATION

Translation of dialogue in standard English

DIALOGUE

A day of housecleaning.

Earl: Did you see this **insignificant object** I found?

Anne: Where did you get that?

Earl: In this box of **various items** your mother's been saving. What a **collection** of junk. For a person who likes everything **extremely clean**, she sure did let everything get dirty.

Anne: Look! Here's my old **table tennis** paddle! And my grandfather's watch! I haven't seen that in years. I always liked the **crossing lines** on the back. Listen. It still works! Hear it **ticking**? It's still in **excellent** shape. I'm so excited that my grandparents are coming here next week. I know they're going to love their new grandchild.

Earl: I just hope they have the energy to play with him.

Anne: Oh, they're both full of **energy**. They absolutely love the **sound** of children around the house, too.

Lesson Eleven - ALLITERATION

Earl finds 'n int'r'sting "knick-knack"

DIALOGUE

A day of housecleaning.

Earl: Did ju see this **knick-knack** I found?

Anne: Where'd ja get that?

Earl: In this box 'a **bric-a-brac** yer mother's been saving. Whad a **mish-mash** 'a junk. Fer a person who likes ev'rything **spic-'n-span**, she sher did led ev'rything get dirdy.

Anne: Look! Here's my old **ping-pong** paddle! An' my gran'father's watch! I haven't seen thad'n years. I always liked the **criss-cross** paddern on the back. Listen. It still works! Hear it going **tick-tock**? It's still 'n **tip-top** shape. I'm so excided that my gran'parents 'r coming here next week. I know they're gonna love their new grandchild.

Earl: I just hope they have thee energy da play with 'im.

Anne: Oh, they're both full 'a **vim-'n-vigor**. They absolutely love the **pidder-padder** of liddle feed aroun' the house, too.

Vocabulary

bric-a-brac *exp.* a group of inexpensive collectible objects, usually displayed in one's home.

  usage example (1): This is some **bric-a-brac** I've collected over the years.

  translation: These are some objects I've collected over the years.

  usage example (2): The burglars stole a lot of **bric-a-brac** from our house. Luckily, they didn't find my jewelry.

  translation: The burglars stole of a lot of insignificant objects from our house. Luckily, they didn't find my jewelry.

criss-cross • **1.** (noun) a pattern or design made of crossing lines • **2.** (verb) to cross.

  usage example (1): Last night, my mother wore a blue dress with a **criss-cross** pattern on the front.

  translation: Last night, my mother wore a blue dress with a design made of crossing lines on the front.

  usage example (2): The top to my sister's bathing suit **criss-crosses** in the back.

  translation: The top to my sister's bathing suit crosses in the back.

knick-knack *exp.* a name given to an insignificant object or trinket; a "thing."

  usage example (1): How long have you been collecting these **knick-knacks**?

  translation: How long have you been collecting these things?

  usage example (2): I brought you a little gift from my vacation. It's just a little **knick-knack** I thought you'd like.

translation: I brought you a little gift from my vacation. It's just a little object I thought you'd like.

VARIATION: **nicknack** *exp.*

mish-mash *exp.* a collection of unrelated items or elements.

usage example (1): At the party last night, they served a **mish-mash** of different foods. The appetizers were Ethiopian, the main course was a French delicacy, the vegetables were prepared Spanish style, and the desserts were all Greek.

translation: At the part last night, they served a variety of different foods. The appetizers were Ethiopian, the main course was a French delicacy, the vegetables were prepared Spanish style, and the desserts were all Greek.

usage example (2): I don't like this painting. The artist used a **mish-mash** of colors. I would have preferred it if he had used different shades of only a few colors.

translation: I don't like this painting. The artist used a variety of unrelated colors. I would have preferred it if he had used different shades of only a few colors.

ping pong *exp.* table tennis (originally a trademark for table tennis equipment).

usage example (1): Do you know how to play **ping pong**?

translation: Do you know to play table tennis?

usage example (2): **Ping pong** is very popular in Japan.

translation: Table tennis is very popular in Japan.

NOTE: **Ping Pong** is a trademark and should be capitalized (although generally it is not).

pitter-patter *exp.* noise made by anything that causes alternating tones (such as rain, footsteps, etc.).

usage example (1): I love the **pitter-patter** of the rain.

translation: I love the sound the rain makes.

usage example (2): Soon, you'll be hearing the **pitter-patter** of little feet at our house. I'm going to be a father!

translation: Soon, you'll be hearing the sound of little feet at our house. I'm going to be a father!

Ah, the "pitter-patter" of little feet...

spic-and-span *exp.* extremely clean.

usage example (1): We have to get the house **spic-and-span** before my relatives come to visit.

translation: We have to get the house completely clean before my relatives come to visit.

usage example (2): I've been cleaning the oven for two hours. It's finally **spic-and-span**.

translation: I've been cleaning the oven for two hours. It's finally very clean.

tick-tock *exp.* the sound made by a clock (usually a pendulum clock).

    usage example (1): The sound of my clock going **tick-tock** kept me awake all night.

    translation: The sound of my clock ticking kept me awake all night.

    usage example (2): What's that loud **tick-tock** sound I hear?

    translation: What's that loud ticking sound I hear?

    VARIATION: **tick-tocking** *exp.*

        usage example: Do you hear that **tick-tocking** coming from your neighbor's house?

        translation: Do you hear that ticking sound coming from your neighbor's house?

tip-top *exp.* the highest degree of excellence.

    usage example (1): I feel **tip-top** today.

    translation: I feel in the most excellent health today.

    usage example (2): My grandmother is always in **tip-top** condition.

    translation: My grandmother is always in the most excellent condition.

vim-and-vigor *exp.* energy, stamina.

    usage example (1): Your mother went hiking with you? She must have lots of **vim-and-vigor**.

    translation: Your mother went hiking with you? She must have lots of energy.

    usage example (2): Don't you want to go skiing with us? Have you lost your **vim-and-vigor**?

    translation: Don't you want to go skiing with us? Have you lost your energy and stamina?

Practice The Vocabulary 📼

(Answers to Lesson 11, p. 270)

A. Choose the correct phrase that best fits the idiom.

1. **What's that pitter-patter sound?**
   - ☐ a. My neighbor must have dropped something heavy.
   - ☐ b. It must be a fire truck passing by.
   - ☐ c. I think it just started to rain.

2. **I've never seen you with such vim-and-vigor!**
   - ☐ a. You must be feeling terribly sick.
   - ☐ b. You must be feeling great.
   - ☐ c. You must be very confused.

3. **What's making that tick-tock sound?**
   - ☐ a. That's the sound of my clock.
   - ☐ b. That's the sound of my dog.
   - ☐ c. That's the sound of my cat.

4. **I'm in tip-top shape.**
   - ☐ a. I have a bad cold.
   - ☐ b. I have no energy.
   - ☐ c. I've never felt better.

5. **My mother gave me a little knick-knack she bought in France.**
   - ☐ a. It was extremely expensive.
   - ☐ b. It was a priceless painting.
   - ☐ c. It was an inexpensive souvenir.

6. **Jeannie used a mish-mash of spices in her fish sauce.**
   - ☐ a. She used only one spice.
   - ☐ b. She didn't use any spices at all.
   - ☐ c. She used many different spices.

7. **Your kitchen is so spic-and-span.**
   - ☐ a. Is it always this clean?
   - ☐ b. Is it always this dirty?
   - ☐ c. Is it always this bright?

B. FILL-IN BLOCKS

Step 1: Fill in the blanks below with the appropriate word from the following list.

Step 2: Using your answers, fill in the blocks on the opposite page (number 3 has been done for you).

brac	mash	tock
cross	pong	top
knack	span	vigor

ACROSS ONLY

1. Dianne gave me this pretty knick- _____ from her trip to Los Angeles.

2. At the concert, we heard a mish- _____ of different styles like jazz, classical, rock, and gospel.

3. Anna collects so much bric-a-_____ that she hardly has any room in her house.

4. I want your bedroom to be spic-and- _____ before our guests arrive.

5. My new dishes have a pretty criss- _____ pattern.

6. Would you like to play a game of ping- _____ ?

7. I don't think my watch is working. I don't hear it going tick- _____ .

8. After being sick for a week, I'm finally in tip- _____ shape.

9. My grandfather is eighty years old and he's still full of vim-and- _____ .

FILL-IN BLOCKS

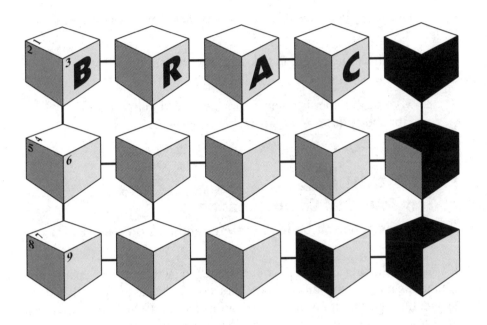

C. Underline the appropriate word that best completes the phrase.

1. Your house is so spic-and-(**spoon**, **spin**, **span**)! I've never seen it this clean.

2. The rain is making a pitter-(**pitter**, **patter**, **pot**) sound on the window.

3. I love collecting little knick-(**knives**, **knacks**, **knats**) from different places that I visit.

4. Sandy has decorated her house in a mish-(**mush**, **mash**, **mat**) of different styles.

5. The top to my sister's bathing suit criss-(**crosses, greases, cruises**) in the back.

6. I've never been healthier. I'm in tip-(**top, tock, tick**) shape.

7. My clock makes a loud tick-(**tip, top, tock**) sound.

8. My grandmother is ninety years old and still has lots of vim-and-(**liquor, vicar, vigor**).

E. DICTATION
Test Your Oral Comprehension
(This dictation can be found in Appendix A on page 280).

If you are following along with your cassette, you will now hear a paragraph containing many of the idioms from this section. The paragraph will be read by a native speaker at normal conversational speed (which may seem fast to you at first). In addition, the words will be pronounced *as you would actually hear them in a conversation,* including many common reductions.

The first time the paragraph is presented, simply listen in order to get accustomed to the speed and heavy use of reductions. The paragraph will then be read again with a pause after each group of words to give you time to write down what you heard. The third time the paragraph is read, follow along with what you have written.

A CLOSER LOOK:
More Two-, Three-, and Four-Word Idioms Beginning with the Same Letter

chit-chat *v. & n.* trivial conversation.

   usage example (1): [as a verb]
      Let's go somewhere and **chit-chat** for a while.

     translation: Let's go somewhere and converse for a while.

   usage example (2): [as a noun]
      The party was fun. There was lots of **chit-chat** and good food.

     translation: The party was fun. There was lots of conversation and good food.

clip-clop *exp.* This refers to the sound made by a horse as it walks on hard ground.

   usage example: Do you hear that **clip-clop** sound? There must be a horse nearby.

     translation: Do you hear that sound a horse makes as it walks? There must be a horse nearby.

ding-dong *n.* This refers to the sound made by a ringing bell.

   usage example: Did you hear that **ding-dong** sound? I think someone is at your front door.

     translation: Did you hear that bell sound? I think someone is at your front door.

fit as a fiddle (to be) *exp.* to be extremely healthy (used primarily by residents of rural areas).

   usage example: I was sick yesterday but today I'm **fit as a fiddle**.

     translation: I was sick yesterday but today I'm in great health.

flip-flop (to) *exp.* to reverse the order of something.

> *usage example (1):* The answer to this mathematical problem isn't 32. It's
> 23. You **flip-flopped** the numbers.
>
> *translation:* The answer to this mathematical problem isn't 32. It's
> 23. You reversed the numbers.
>
> **ALSO:** **flip-flop (to do a)** *exp.* to change dramatically.
>
>> *usage example:* My mom did a real **flip flop** yesterday.
>> She said I couldn't go to the party under
>> any circumstances. Today she said that
>> I could go!

goochy-goo *exp.* These words are used to indicate that someone is being
tickled.

> *usage example:* Your baby is so cute! **Goochy-goo**!
>
> *translation:* Your baby is so cute! Tickle, tickle!
>
> **VARIATION (1):** **goochy-goochy-goo** *exp.*
> **VARIATION (2):** **coochy-[coochy] coo** *exp.*

jingle-jangle *exp.* The sound made by metallic objects rubbing against
each other.

> *usage example:* Do you have keys in your pocket? I hear a **jingle-
> jangle** sound as you walk.
>
> *translation:* Do you have keys in your pocket? I hear a jingling
> sound as you walk.

junk-food junkie *exp.* a person who loves unhealthful food such as
candies, cookies, fried foods, etc.

> *usage example:* I admit that I'm a **junk-food junkie**. I could eat
> cookies all day!
>
> *translation:* I admit that I love unhealthful food. I could eat cookies
> all day!

riff-raff *exp.* dishonorable people.

> *usage example:* You like these people? They're nothing but **riff-raff**!
>
> *translation:* You like these people? They're all totally dishonorable.

right-as-rain *exp.* perfectly fine (used only by natives of the southern part of the U.S.).

> *usage example:* Everything's **right-as-rain**!
>
> *translation:* Everything's going perfectly fine!

see-saw *n.* A recreational device on which two children, seated at opposite ends of a long plank balanced in the middle, alternately ride up and down as each exerts his/her weight.

> *usage example:* Let's go play on the **see-saw**!
>
> **SYNONYM:** **teeter-totter** *n.*

ship-shape *exp.* very orderly and clean (originally a nautical term).

> *usage example:* Your house is really **ship-shape**. My house is always so messy.
>
> *translation:* Your house is really orderly and clean. My house is always so messy.

sing-song *exp.* alternating up and down in pitch.

> *usage example:* Italian and Chinese are very **sing-song** languages.
>
> *translation:* Italian and Chinese are very musical languages.

yick-yack *exp.* to talk or chatter meaninglessly.

> *usage example:* Every time I see Jim, all he ever does is **yick-yack**!
>
> *translation:* Every time I see Jim, all he ever does is talk and talk about nothing!
>
> **VARIATION (1):** **yickety-yack** *exp.*
>
> **VARIATION (2):** **yackety-yack** *exp.*
>
> **VARIATION (3):** **yack-yack** *exp.*

Tom is "going toe-to-toe"
with everyone!

Lesson Twelve - REPEATING WORDS

Tom is "going toe-to-toe" with everyone

DIALOGUE

Don and Paul are talking about one of their co-workers.

_____

Don: **More and more**, people are having trouble **seeing eye-to-eye** with Tom. I always thought he was a great guy **through-and-through** but lately he's been a real **so-and-so**. People are even starting to wonder if he's **on the up-and-up**.

Paul: I've told him that **over-and-over**. Frankly, I think he really enjoys **going toe-to-toe** with everyone.

Don: He sure does have an **out-and-out** bad temper! If you don't agree with him, he starts screaming!

Paul: Maybe he just needs some **R-and-R**. I think I need to have a **tête-à-tête** with him today.

Lesson Twelve - REPEATING WORDS

Translation of dialogue in standard English

DIALOGUE

Don and Paul are talking about one of their co-workers.

Don: **Increasingly often**, people are having trouble **agreeing** with Tom. I always thought he was a great guy **in every respect** but lately he's been a real **[replacement for any vulgar word]**. People are even starting to wonder if he's **honest**.

Paul: I've told him that **many times**. Frankly, I think he really enjoys **debating** with everyone.

Don: He sure does have a **really** bad temper! If you don't agree with him, he starts screaming!

Paul: Maybe he just needs some **rest and recreation**. I think I need to have a **private discussion** with him today.

Lesson Twelve - REPEATING WORDS

Dialogue in slang as it would be heard

Tom is "going toe-da-toe" with ev'ryone

DIALOGUE

Don 'n Paul 'r talking about one 'a their co-workers.

Don: **More 'n more**, people 'r having trouble **seeing eye-da-eye** with Tom. I always thod 'e was a great guy **through-'n-through** but lately he's been a real **so-'n-so**. People 'r even starding ta wonder if 'e's **on thee up-'n-up**.

Paul: I've told 'im thad **over-'n-over**. Frankly, I think 'e really enjoys **going toe-da-toe** with ev'ryone.

Don: He sure does have 'n **out-'n-out** bad temper! If ya don' agree with 'im, 'e starts screaming!

Paul: Maybe 'e jus' needs s'm **R-'n-R**. I think I need ta have a **tade-à-tate** with 'im t'day.

Vocabulary

NOTE: *There is a lot of argument among copyeditors and dictionaries whether many of the following repeating words should be hyphenated or not. Therefore, don't be surprised that throughout your journey into American-English, you may encounter some differences in how these types of expressions are written.*

eye-to-eye (to see) *exp.* to be in agreement.

   usage example (1): We don't **see eye-to-eye** on how to raise children.

   translation: We don't agree on how to raise children.

   usage example (2): My boss and I don't **see eye-to-eye** on how a company should be run.

   translation: My boss and I don't agree on how a company should be run.

more and more *exp.* increasingly often.

   usage example (1): **More and more**, people are moving to California.

   translation: Increasingly often, people are moving to California.

   usage example (2): There's a lot of crime in our city. It's happening **more and more**.

   translation: There's a lot of crime in our city. It's happening increasingly often.

   NOTE (1): As seen above, when followed by a comma (or pause), the expression *"more and more"* means "increasingly often." However, if not followed by a comma (or pause), the expression means "an increasing amount." For example:
   More and more, *people are moving to California.*
   Increasingly often, people are moving to California.
   More and more *people are moving to California.*
   An increasing number of people are moving to California.

NOTE (2): When followed by a comma (or pause), the expression *"less and less"* means "increasingly seldom." However, if not followed by a comma (or pause), the expression means "a decreasing amount." For example:

Less and less, *people are buying cars.*
Decreasingly often, people are buying cars.
Less and less *people are buying new cars.*
A decreasing number of people are buying new cars.

out-and-out *exp.* complete, total (may be used to modify a noun or a verb).

usage example (1): He's an **out-and-out** liar!

translation: He's a complete liar!

usage example (2): He **out-and-out** lied!

translation: He completely lied!

over-and-over *exp.* repeatedly.

usage example (1): I've told you **over-and-over** to take your shoes off before you walk on the new carpet.

translation: I've told you repeatedly to take your shoes off before you walk on the new carpet.

usage example (2): I've told you five times how to use this computer program, but you keep making the same mistakes **over-and-over**!

translation: I've told you five times how to use this computer program, but you keep making the same mistakes repeatedly!

VARIATION: **over-and-over again** *exp.*

R-and-R *exp.* (originally military lingo) rest and recreation (or rest and relaxation).

usage example (1): I've been working hard. I need some **R-and-R**.

translation: I've been working hard. I need some rest and recreation.

usage example (2): You look very tired today. I think you need some **R-and-R**.

translation: You look very tired today. I think you need some rest and recreation.

NOTE: The expression *"R and R"* is always pronounced *R 'n R*.

David's idea of "R 'n R."

so-and-so *exp.* • **1.** a replacement for the name of a person; someone • **2.** a euphemistic replacement for any vulgar or obscene noun pertaining to a person.

usage example (1): What would you do if **so-and-so** approached you and demanded all your money?

translation: What would you do if someone approached you and demanded all your money?

usage example (2): How can you let that **so-and-so** say such mean things to you?

translation: How can you let that [vulgar or obscene noun pertaining to a person] say such mean things to you?

NOTE: The expression *"so-and-so"* is always pronounced *so-'n-so.*

tête-à-tête *exp.* (French) a private conversation between two people.

usage example (1): The boss is having a **tête-à-tête** with Richard. Do you think he's going to get fired?

translation: The boss is having a private conversation with Richard. Do you think he's going to get fired?

usage example (2): We need to have a **tête-à-tête** right now. Please come into my office.

translation: We need to have a private conversation right now. Please come into my office.

NOTE: This expression comes from French meaning a "head-to-head." In France, the pronunciation is *"tet-a-tet."* However in America, it is commonly pronounced *"tate-a-tate."*

through-and-through *exp.* in every respect, completely.

usage example (1): Kim's an actress **through-and-through**. She was in her first play at age five and still loves the theater.

translation: Kim's an actress in every respect. She was in her first play at age five and still loves the theater.

usage example (2): The president of our school is a leader **through-and-through**.

translation: The president of our school is a leader in every respect.

toe-to-toe (to go) *exp.* to debate or compete.

usage example (1): Joe and Ann **went toe to toe** on the issue of women's rights.

translation: Joe and Ann debated the issue of women's rights.

usage example (2): The two best soccer teams in the world will be **going toe-to-toe** tomorrow. You won't want to miss it!

translation: The two best soccer teams in the world will be competing tomorrow. You won't want to miss it!

up-and-up (to be on the) *exp.* to be candid and honest.

usage example (1): Do you think that politician is **on the up-and-up**?

translation: Do you think that politician is candid and honest?

usage example (2): That salesman told me that this is the best car for my money. Do you think he's being **on the up-and-up**?

translation: That salesman told me that this is the best car for my money. Do you think he's being candid and honest?

Do you think this politician is **"on the up and up?"**

Practice The Vocabulary 📼

(Answers to Lesson 12, p. 271)

A. Are the following idioms used correctly or incorrectly?

1. **More and more**, people are moving to the country.
   ☐ correct   ☐ incorrect

2. Steve and I don't see **eye-to-eye** on how to do this job. We always agree on everything.
   ☐ correct   ☐ incorrect

3. He's an **out-and-out** thief! He steals other people's possessions all the time!
   ☐ correct   ☐ incorrect

4. She makes the same mistakes **over-and-over**.
   ☐ correct   ☐ incorrect

5. You look very rested. Maybe you need some **R-and-R**.
   ☐ correct   ☐ incorrect

6. Do you believe what that **so-and-so** did to me?
   ☐ correct   ☐ incorrect

7. This meal looks great! What a **tête-à-tête**!
   ☐ correct   ☐ incorrect

8. Ed and Barbara went **toe-to-toe** all night. You should have seen them dance!
   ☐ correct   ☐ incorrect

B. Choose the correct answer from the list below.

more and more
over-and-over
R and R
so-and-so

tête-à-tête
through-and-through
to go toe-to-toe
up-and-up

1. increasingly often.

   Answer: _____

2. in every respect, completely.

   Answer: _____

3. candid and honest.

   Answer: _____

4. **1.** a replacement for the name of a person; someone •
   2. a euphemistic replacement for any vulgar or obscene
   noun pertaining to a person.

   Answer: _____

5. repeatedly.

   Answer: _____

6. (originally military lingo) rest and recreation.

   Answer: _____

7. (French) a private conversation between two people.

   Answer: _____

8. to debate or compete (with someone).

   Answer: _____

C. Underline the appropriate words that best complete the phrase.

1. I don't agree with you. I'm afraid we just don't see (**mouth-to-mouth, out-and-out, eye-to-eye**).

2. I've told you (**toe-to-toe, over-and-over, tête-à-tête**) not to use my bicycle without asking first.

3. (**Through-and-through, more and more, toe-to-toe**), people are complimenting me on my clothes. It happens almost every day!

4. Larry and I had a (**tête-à-tête, more and more, so-and-so**) which lasted an hour. It was very productive. We need to have more meetings like that in the future.

5. You look exhausted. I think you need some (**R-and-R, eye-to-eye, up-and-up**).

6. She told you I stole her money? She's an (**eye-to-eye, out-and-out, more and more**) liar!

7. Irene is honest (**through-and-through, out-and-out, eye-to-eye**).

8. I don't trust him. I don't think he's on the (**up-and-up, so-and-so, R-and-R**).

9. I don't like him. He's a real (**so-and-so, more and more, R-and-R**).

10. You never agree with anyone. You must like going (**over-and- over, eye-to-eye, toe-to-toe**) with people.

D. Choose the definition of the words in boldface.

1. He's a good worker **through-and-through**.
   - ☐ a. in every respect, completely
   - ☐ b. occasionally
   - ☐ c. in the mornings

2. Todd **went toe-to-toe** with Cindy yesterday.
   - ☐ a. took a walk
   - ☐ b. debated
   - ☐ c. went dancing

3. Our new boss is a real **so-and-so**.
   - ☐ a. wonderful person
   - ☐ b. rich person
   - ☐ c. (a euphemistic replacement for any vulgar or obscene noun pertaining to a person)

4. He hit me **over-and-over**!
   - ☐ a. on the head
   - ☐ b. repeatedly
   - ☐ c. with his fist

5. Donna is an **out-and-out** traitor. She told everyone my secret.
   - ☐ a. complete, total
   - ☐ b. mild
   - ☐ c. extraverted

6. **More and more**, I get nervous when I have to give speeches.
   - ☐ a. increasingly often
   - ☐ b. decreasingly often
   - ☐ c. sometimes

7. Jim and I don't **see eye-to-eye** on anything.
   - ☐ a. disagree
   - ☐ b. agree
   - ☐ c. count

8. I've been working too hard. I think I need some **R-and-R**.
   - ☐ a. rest and recreation
   - ☐ b. rest and running
   - ☐ c. rest and rebuilding

E. DICTATION 📼
Test Your Oral Comprehension
(This dictation can be found in Appendix A on page 281).

If you are following along with your cassette, you will now hear a paragraph containing many of the idioms from this section. The paragraph will be read by a native speaker at normal conversational speed (which may seem fast to you at first). In addition, the words will be pronounced *as you would actually hear them in a conversation,* including many common reductions.

The first time the paragraph is presented, simply listen in order to get accustomed to the speed and heavy use of reductions. The paragraph will then be read again with a pause after each group of words to give you time to write down what you heard. The third time the paragraph is read, follow along with what you have written.

A CLOSER LOOK:
More Repeating Words

If you've ever been accused of repeating yourself, you're in good company. The following is a list of repeating words which may seem to go *"on and on"* at first. However, these words shouldn't be *"pooh-poohed"* since they certainly occur *"again and again"* in daily conversations.

again and again *exp.* repeatedly.

> *usage example:* I've told you **again and again** to stop bothering me!

> *translation:* I've told you repeatedly to stop bothering me!

boo-boo *exp.* (baby talk) injury.

> *usage example:* Did you get a **boo-boo** when you fell down?

> *translation:* Did you get injured when you fell down?

NOTE: As just demonstrated, when the sound *"boo"* is repeated, it takes on the meaning of "injury." However, as a single syllable *("Boo!")*, it becomes an interjection used to scare someone:

usage example: Stephanie was hiding behind the door. As soon as I walked by, she jumped out and yelled **"Boo!"**

bye-bye *exp.* (commonly pronounced *"ba-bye"*) good-bye.

usage example: **Bye-bye**! See you tomorrow.

translation: Good-bye. See you tomorrow.

NOTE: Young children are commonly told to *"wave bye-bye,"* a phrase applied *only* to children. However, adults do frequently used the phrase *"bye-bye"* with other adults, especially on the telephone.

cheek-to-cheek *exp.* one person's cheek pressed up against another person's cheek.

usage example: I don't think they're just friends. I saw John and Lisa dancing **cheek-to-cheek** all night!

translation: I don't think they're just friends. I saw John and Lisa dancing with their cheeks pressed up against each other's all night!

choo-choo *n.* (baby talk) train.

usage example: Look at the big **choo-choo**!

translation: Look at the big train!

VARIATION: **choo-choo train** *n.*

door-to-door (to go) *exp.* to solicit each house in a neighborhood (in hopes of selling a product).

usage example: The salesperson went **door-to-door** trying to sell brushes.

translation: The salesperson went to each house in the neighborhood trying to sell brushes.

> **NOTE:** **door-to-door salesperson** *n.* a merchant who goes to each house in a neighborhood trying to selling products.

ear-to-ear *exp.* from one ear to the other.

> *usage example:* When I walked in, my mother was smiling from **ear-to-ear**.

> *translation:* When I walked in, my mother had an enormous smile on her face.

face-to-face *exp.* in person.

> *usage example:* I've been looking forward to meeting you **face-to-face**.

> *translation:* I've been looking forward to meeting you in person.

frou-frou *exp.* elaborate.

> *usage example:* Did you see the way Susie decorated her house? It's too **frou-frou** for me.

> *translation:* Did you see the way Susie decorated her house? It's too elaborate for me.

ga-ga over someone or something (to go) *exp.* to become infatuated by someone or something.

> *usage example:* The first time I saw Rachelle, I went **ga-ga** over her. Isn't she beautiful?

> *translation:* The first time I saw Rachelle, I became infatuated with her. Isn't she beautiful?

> **NOTE:** You may occasionally hear *"ga-ga"* used in conjunction with *"goo-goo."* *"Goo-goo, ga-ga!"* is commonly used by adults as they talk to babies in an effort to imitate the sound they make.

goochy-goochy *exp.* tickle, tickle.

> *usage example:* I'm going to tickle you! **Goochy-goochy**!

translation: I'm going to tickle you! Tickle, tickle!

NOTE: This phrase is commonly used by someone who is tickling someone else.

VARIATION (1): **goochy-goochy-goo** *exp.*

VARIATION (2): **coochy-coochy-coo** *exp.*

ha-ha *exp.* used to indicate laughter (usually sarcastically).

usage example: "What did you think of my joke?"
"**Ha-ha**. Very funny."

ALSO: **Ha-ha!** *exp.* used to indicate contempt for someone else's misfortune.

usage example: **Ha-ha**! I won and you lost!

SYNONYM: **hee-hee** *exp.*

hand-in-hand (to walk) *exp.* to walk while holding hands with someone.

usage example: They must be very good friends. They're **walking hand-in-hand**.

translation: They must be very good friends. They're walking and holding each other's hands.

ALSO: **to go hand-in-hand** *exp.* to go together.

usage example: Do you think that being rich and being happy **go hand-in- hand**?

translation: Do you think that being rich and being happy go together?

hand-to-hand combat *exp.* fighting with one's hands (as opposed to using weapons).

usage example: The two teams got involved in **hand-to-hand combat**.

translation: The two teams fought each other by use of their hands.

head-to-head (to go) *exp.* to fight verbally or physically (like two rams that battle by thrusting their heads against each other).

> *usage example:* Mark and Paul went **head-to-head** for an hour over who should be allowed to go on vacation first.
>
> *translation:* Mark and Paul fought for an hour over who should be allowed to go on vacation first.

heart-to-heart *exp.* an honest and open conversation.

> *usage example:* We need to have a **heart-to-heart** about sex.
>
> *translation:* We need to have an honest and open conversation about sex.

"Hip-hip-hooray!" *exp.* a common cheer.

> *usage example:* Let's hear it for our hero! **Hip-hip-hooray**!

lu-lu (to be a) *exp.* said of something impressive.

> *usage example:* How did you get that black eye? What a **lu-lu**!
>
> *translation:* How did you get that black eye? How impressive!

muu-muu *n.* a long cool one-piece dress (originally worn by women in Hawaii - pronounced "moo-moo").

> *usage example:* I bought this **muu-muu** in Hawaii. It'll be perfect to wear when I go to parties this summer.
>
> *translation:* I bought this cool long one-piece dress in Hawaii. It'll be perfect to wear when I go to parties this summer.

mouth-to-mouth *exp.* (short for *"mouth-to-mouth resuscitation"*) a resuscitation technique used on someone who has stopped breathing - the technique consists of pressing the rescuer's mouth against the victim's mouth and blowing air into his/her lungs.

> *usage example:* I had to give **mouth-to-mouth** to my little brother when he fell into the swimming pool and stopped breathing.

translation: I had to resuscitate my little brother when he fell into the swimming pool and stopped breathing.

"Naughty, naughty!" *exp.* a phrase used primarily by parents when scolding a disobedient child.

> *usage example:* **Naughty, naughty!** I told you not to touch that!

neck-and-neck (to be) *exp.* to be even in a race.

> *usage example:* The two runners are **neck-and-neck**. I wonder who will finally be the winner!

> *translation:* The two runners are even. I wonder who will finally be the winner!

no-no *n.* (used by parents when talking to a child) not permitted.

> *usage example:* Eating ice cream in the living room is a **no-no**!

> *translation:* Eating ice cream in the living room is not permitted!

> **NOTE (1):** Adults frequently use this expression among themselves as well. For example:

> *usage example:* Being late is a big **no-no** in this office.

> **NOTE (2):** Other synonyms for *"no"* would be incorrect in this expression, such as *"nope-nope," "nah-nah,"* etc. Additionally, this expression does not work with *"yes."* Therefore, *"yes-yes," "yep-yep," "uh-huh, uh-huh,"* etc. would all be incorrect usage.

on-and-on (to go) *exp.* to talk incessantly.

> *usage example:* Lisa **goes on-and-on** about how she wants to be a big movie star some day.

> *translation:* Lisa talks incessantly about how she wants to be a big movie star some day.

one-by-one *exp.* one person or thing at a time.

> *usage example:* I want you to fold your shirts carefully **one-by-one**.

> *translation:* I want you to fold your shirts carefully one at a time.

pee-pee (to go) *exp.* (originally baby talk but also used in jest by adults) to urinate.

    usage example: I have **to go pee-pee** before we leave.

    translation: I have to go urinate before we leave.

pom-pom *n.* a ball of wool, feathers, or strips of colored paper used as decoration and by cheerleaders (also spelled *"pom-pon"*).

    usage example: The cheerleaders were waving their **pom-poms** as they cheered the soccer team.

    translation: The cheerleaders were waving decorative balls of colored paper as they cheered the soccer team.

pooh-pooh (to go) *n.* (baby talk - pronounced *"POO-poo"* with the emphasis on the first *"poo"*) to defecate.

    usage example: I think Tessa just **went pooh-pooh** in her diapers.

    translation: I think Tessa just defecated in her diapers.

    ALSO: **to pooh-pooh something** *exp.* (pronounced *"poo-POO"* with the emphasis on the second *"poo"*) to reject something.

        usage example: The boss **pooh-poohed** my idea of hiring Steve.

        translation: The boss rejected my idea of hiring Steve.

same old-same old *exp.* same as usual.

    usage example: "How's everything going?"
                              "Same old, same old."

    translation: "How's everything going?"
                              "Same as usual."

so-so *exp.* neither very good nor very bad, passable.

    usage example: "How did your job interview go?"
                              "So-so."

    translation: "How did your job interview go?"
                              "It was passable."

such-and-such *exp.* not yet determined.

> *usage example:* We'll all meet tomorrow at **such-and-such** a time.

> *translation:* We'll all meet tomorrow at a time to be determined later.

ta-ta *exp.* (pronounced "ta-TA" with the emphasis on the second "ta") good-bye.

> *usage example:* See you tomorrow. **Ta-ta**!

> *translation:* See you tomorrow. Good-bye!

tee-tee (to go) *exp.* (baby talk) to urinate.

> *usage example:* Do you have **to go tee-tee**?

> *translation:* Do you have to go urinate?

tom-tom *exp.* a small drum beaten with the hands.

> *usage example:* My parents gave my little brother a set of **tom-toms** for his birthday. He plays them all day long!

> *translation:* My parents gave my little brother a set of small drums for his birthday. He plays them all day long!

tum-tum *exp.* (baby talk) stomach.

> *usage example:* You ate lots of ice cream today. Is your **tum-tum** full?

> *translation:* You ate lots of ice cream today. Is your stomach full?

two-by-two *exp.* one person next to the other.

> *usage example:* I want you all to form a line **two-by-two**.

> *translation:* I want you all to form a line one person next to the other.

> **SYNONYM:** **side-by-side** *exp.*

yum yum *exp.* used to indicate that something is delicious.

> *usage example:* "Would you like a piece of chocolate cake?" "**Yum yum**! I love chocolate cake!"

> *translation:* "Would you like a piece of chocolate cake?" "That sounds delicious! I love chocolate cake!"

"When it rains, it pours"

Lesson Thirteen - PROVERBS

When it rains, it pours

DIALOGUE

Lots of mail!

Lee: Look at all this mail I got today. **When it rains, it pours**! Here's a letter from Patricia.

Ben: I didn't think you were friends anymore.

Lee: I decided **to let bygones be bygones**. It's about time I got a letter from her! She hasn't written to me since she left for Paris last year. **Out of sight, out of mind**.

Ben: She used to tell me constantly how much she valued our friendship but she was never there when I needed her. **Actions speak louder than words**.

Lee: Once I let her borrow my car for an hour and she used it all day! **Give her an inch, she'll take a mile**. So, what does her letter say?

Ben: She says she ate snails for the first time! Well, I suppose **when in Rome, do as the Romans**. She says that they were delicious.

Lee: **There's no accounting for taste**.

Ben: She also says that she fell in love with some guy who is living in England for a year. She's upset because he only writes to her once every two months! Interesting how **the shoe's on the other foot**!

Lesson Thirteen - PROVERBS

Translation of dialogue  in standard English

DIALOGUE

Lots of mail!

Lee: Look at all this mail I got today. **When an event occurs, it occurs with great intensity**! Here's a letter from Patricia.

Ben: I didn't think you were friends anymore.

Lee: I decided **to forget what happened in the past**. It's about time I got a letter from her! She hasn't written to me since she left for Paris last year. **If someone is not in sight, he/she is forgotten**.

Ben: She used to tell me constantly how much she valued our friendship but she was never there when I needed her. **Actions are more meaningful than words**.

Lee: Once I let her borrow my car for an hour and she used it all day! **If you give her a little of something, she'll try to take a lot more**. So, what does her letter say?

Ben: She says she ate snails for the first time! Well, I suppose **one must adopt the habits of the local people**. She says that they were delicious.

Lee: **There's no explanation for people's likes and dislikes**.

Ben: She also says that she fell in love with some guy who is living in England for a year. She's upset because he only writes to her once every two months! Interesting how **she's suffering the same thing she makes other people experience**!

Lesson Thirteen - PROVERBS

Dialogue in slang as it would be heard

When it rains, it pours

DIALOGUE

Lots 'a mail!

Lee: Look 'it all this mail I got t'day. **When it rains, it pours**! Here's a ledder from P'trisha.

Ben: I didn' think you were frenz anymore.

Lee: I decided **ta let bygones be bygones**. It's about time I godda ledder from 'er! She hasn't written ta me since she lef' fer Paris last year. **Outta side, oudda mind**.

Ben: She use' ta tell me constantly how much she valued are fren'ship but she was never there when I needed 'er. **Actions speak louder th'n words**.

Lee: Once I let 'er borrow my car fer an hour an' she used it all day! **Give 'er an inch, she'll take a mile**. So, wha' does 'er ledder say?

Ben: She says she ate snails fer the firs' time! Well, I suppose **when in Rome, do as the Romans**. She says that they were delicious.

Lee: **There's no accoun'ing fer taste**.

Ben: She also says that she fell 'n love with some guy who's living in Englan' fer a year. She's upset b'cause 'e only writes to 'er once every two months! Int'resting how **the shoe's on thee other foot**!

Vocabulary

"Actions speak louder than words" *exp.* "Prove what you say by your actions."

> *usage example:* You always tell me what a good friend I am but every time I need your help, you're always too busy. If I'm really a good friend of yours, show me. **Actions speak louder than words**.

> *translation:* You always tell me what a good friend I am but every time I need your help, you're always too busy. If I'm really a good friend of yours, show me. Prove what you say by your actions.

"Give someone an inch, he/she will take a mile" *exp.* "If you give someone a little of something, he/she will try to take a lot more."

> *usage example:* I let my sister borrow my dress for the evening. Now she wants to take it with her on vacation for a week! **Give her an inch, she'll take a mile**.

> *translation:* I let my sister borrow my dress for the evening. Now she wants to take it with her on vacation for a week! If you give her a little of something, she'll try to take a lot more.

> **NOTE:** This expression may simply be shortened to: **"Give someone an inch"** since the rest of the expression is merely inferred.

"Let bygones be bygones" *exp.* "Let's forget what happened in the past (and look toward the future)."

usage example: I know you had a big fight with Julie a long time ago. Maybe it's time to **let bygones be bygones** and be friends again.

translation: I know you had a big fight with Julie a long time ago. Maybe it's time to forget about what happened in the past and be friends again.

"Out of sight, out of mind" *exp.* "That which you don't see, you don't think about."

usage example: I haven't received a letter from her in over four months and she's my best friend! **Out of sight, out of mind**.

translation: I haven't received a letter from her in over four months and she's my best friend! If I'm not in front of her, she doesn't think of me.

"There's no accounting for taste" *exp.* "There is no explanation for people's likes and dislikes.

usage example: Do you believe that Mike bought that horrible painting? One thing's for sure. **There's no accounting for taste**.

translation: Do you believe that Mike bought that horrible painting? One thing's for sure. There is no explanation for people's likes and dislikes.

"The shoe's on the other foot" *exp.* "The situation is reversed" (said when someone is forced to suffer the same situation that he/she has caused someone else to experience).

usage example: David's horrible old boss is now David's employee! Suddenly **the shoe is on the other foot**.

translation: David's horrible old boss is now David's employee! Suddenly the situation is reversed.

David's ex-boss   David

Suddenly, *the shoe is on the other foot.*

"When in Rome, do as the Romans [do]" *exp.* "One must adopt the habits of the local people."

> *usage example:* I ate raw fish when I went to Japan. I figured "**when in Rome, do as the Romans [do]**."

> *translation:* I ate raw fish when I went to Japan. I figured when you travel, practice the same customs as the natives.

> **VARIATION:** This expression may simply be shortened to: **"When in Rome"** since the rest of the expression is merely inferred.

"When it rains, it pours" *exp.* "When an event occurs, it occurs with great intensity or frequency."

> *usage example:* I got invited to ten parties tonight! **When it rains, it pours**!

> *translation:* I got invited to ten parties tonight! When an event occurs, it occurs with great intensity!

> **VARIATION:** **"It never rains, but it pours"** *exp.*

Practice The Vocabulary 📼

(Answers to Lesson 13, p. 272)

A. Underline the word that best completes the phrase.

1. My best friend moved to Los Angeles two years ago and never sends me any letters. Out of (**sight, view, vision**), out of mind.

2. I got five job interviews in one day. When it (**hails, snows, rains**), it pours!

3. When I visited Paris, I drank wine with my lunch and dinner. When in (**Rome, Paris, Italy**), do as the (**Romans, Parisians, Italians**) [do].

4. Several years ago, Todd and I had a big fight and stopped speaking to each other. We've finally decided to let (**bylaws, bygones, biplanes**) be bygones and be friends again.

5. Stop telling her how much you love her. Show her! (**Contractions, Reactions, Actions**) speak louder than words.

6. You're finally experiencing what you made me tolerate for so many years. So, how does it feel to have the shoe on the other (**toe, foot, head**)?

7. Did you see the ugly dress Barbara was wearing? I guess there's no accounting for (**taste, smell, hearing**).

8. I asked Jill to replace me as president during my vacation. While I was gone, she changed all the rules! Give her an inch, she'll take a (**kilometer, foot, mile**).

B. Complete the idioms by choosing the appropriate word from the list below.

bygones	**Romans**
mile	**shoe**
mind	**taste**
pours	**words**

1. If you really want to help us, don't just talk about it. Do something. Actions speak louder than _____ .

2. I told Keith that he could use my computer for an hour. Now he wants to use it every day! Give him an inch, he'll take a _____ .

3. When I went to Japan, I used chopsticks. When in Rome, do as the _____ [do].

4. Every time I asked for your help, you always said you were too busy. Now you need me to help you. Suddenly the _____'s on the other foot!

5. Let's let bygones be _____ and be friends again.

6. When Jim and I are together, we're best friends. But when he goes out of town, he never thinks of me. Out of sight, out of _____ .

7. I thought I was going to be bored tonight, then eight of my friends called to invite me to parties! When it rains, it _____ !

8. How could he wear such an ugly tie? There's no accounting for _____ .

C. CONTEXT EXERCISE
Choose the best idiom from the right column that goes with the phrase in the left column.

☐ 1. You got accepted to twelve universities today?

A. **There's no accounting for taste.**

☐ 2. Margaret spent a hundred dollars on that ugly dress?

B. **Actions speak louder than words.**

☐ 3. I know we haven't spoken to each other for two years, but I'd like to be friends again.

C. **Suddenly, the shoe is on the other foot.**

☐ 4. The vice president of the company was demoted to secretary and his secretary is now the vice president!

D. **Out of sight, out of mind.**

☐ 5. When I travel, I always like to eat the same food as the natives.

E. **Let's let bygones be bygones.**

☐ 6. Kim takes advantage of every situation.

F. **When it rains, it pours!**

☐ 7. Don't just tell me what a good worker you are, show me.

G. **Give her an inch, she'll take a mile.**

☐ 8. When Joe and I worked together, we were great friends. Now that he found another job, he never calls me.

H. **I believe that when in Rome, do as the Romans [do].**

E. DICTATION 📼
Test Your Oral Comprehension
(This dictation can be found in Appendix A on page 281).

If you are following along with your cassette, you will now hear a paragraph containing many of the idioms from this section. The paragraph will be read by a native speaker at normal conversational speed (which may seem fast to you at first). In addition, the words will be pronounced *as you would actually hear them in a conversation,* including many common reductions.

The first time the paragraph is presented, simply listen in order to get accustomed to the speed and heavy use of reductions. The paragraph will then be read again with a pause after each group of words to give you time to write down what you heard. The third time the paragraph is read, follow along with what you have written.

A CLOSER LOOK:
More Popular Proverbs

"A friend in need is a friend indeed" *exp.* "A friend who is helpful during times of difficulty is a true friend."

> *usage example:* Your best friend could really use your help. Remember, **a friend in need is a friend indeed**.

> *translation:* Your best friend could really use your help. Remember, a friend who is helpful during times of difficulty is a true friend.

"A little knowledge is a dangerous thing" *exp.* "Having only a little information regarding a certain subject could lead to trouble."

> *usage example:* Paul is going to try and fix his own car? He only read one chapter of his auto mechanics book! He's about to prove that **a little knowledge is a dangerous thing**.

translation: Paul is going to try and fix his own car? He only read one chapter of his auto mechanics book! He's about to prove that having a little information about something could lead to trouble.

"A penny saved is a penny earned" *exp.* "It's important to be frugal."

usage example: If I buy shoes at this store, it will cost less than if I bought them at the other store. I know I'll only be saving a few cents, but **a penny saved is a penny earned**.

translation: If I buy shoes at this store, it will cost less than if I bought them at the other store. I know I'll only be saving a few cents, but it's important to be frugal.

"A watched pot never boils" *exp.* "If you wait for something to happen, it never will."

usage example: I know you're waiting for Mark's telephone call, but you can't just sit next to the telephone all day. You know what they say, "**A watched pot never boils**." Why don't you go do something to keep yourself busy?

translation: I know you're waiting for Mark's telephone call, but you can't just sit next to the telephone all day. You know what they say, "If you wait for something to happen, it never will." Why don't you go do something to keep yourself busy?

"Absence makes the heart grow fonder" *exp.* "People, places, and things become more valued the longer they are absent."

usage example: When your boyfriend comes back from his vacation, he'll be even more in love with you. Remember, **absence makes the heart grow fonder**.

translation: When your boyfriend comes back from his vacation, he'll be even more in love with you. Remember, people, places, and things become more valued the longer they are absent.

"All's fair in love and war" *exp.* "When two people are fighting to win the love of someone else, there are no rules of fair play."

usage example: Mark wants Laura to fall in love with him instead of Tim. So, he lied and told Laura that Tim used to be in prison! I guess **all's fair in love and war**.

translation: Mark wants Laura to fall in love with him instead of Tim. So, he lied and told Laura that Tim used to be in prison! I guess when two people are fighting to win the love of someone else, there are no rules of fair play.

"All's well that ends well" *exp.* "As long as there is a happy outcome to a situation, the struggle to achieve it was worthwhile."

usage example: Mandy lost her house in the fire, but it looks like she'll be able to rebuild an even bigger and better one! **All's well that ends well**.

translation: Mandy lost her house in the fire, but it looks like she'll be able to rebuild an even bigger and better one! As long as there is a happy outcome to a situation, the struggle to achieve it was worthwhile.

"Beauty is only skin deep" *exp.* "The true measure of beauty is by someone's goodness, not by his or her looks."

usage example: Lana may be beautiful, but she's a terrible person. She sure does prove that **beauty is only skin deep**.

translation: Lana may be beautiful, but she's a terrible person. She sure does prove that the true measure of beauty is by someone's goodness, not his or her looks.

"Beggars can't be choosers" *exp.* "People who are given something for free can't be selective."

usage example: Peter forgot to bring his lunch when we went on our hike, so I offered him some of mine. When I gave him my chicken sandwich, he said he wanted my tuna sandwich instead. I told him that **beggars can't be choosers** and that he could have the chicken sandwich or nothing!

translation: Peter forgot to bring his lunch when we went on our hike, so I offered him some of mine. When I gave him my chicken sandwich, he said he wanted my tuna sandwich instead. I told him that people who are given something for free can't be selective and that he could have the chicken sandwich or nothing!

"Better late than never" *exp.* "It's better to do something late than not to do it at all."

usage example: Although it's late, I wanted to give you this birthday gift. **Better late than never**!

translation: Although it's late, I wanted to give you this birthday gift. It's better to do something late than not to do it at all!

"Better safe than sorry" *exp.* "It's better to do something cautiously or else you may suffer the consequences later."

usage example: I know the piano is far from where we're going to be painting, but we'd better cover it anyway. **Better safe than sorry**.

translation: I know the piano is far from where we're going to be painting, but we'd better cover it anyway. It's better to do something cautiously or else you may suffer the consequences later.

"Birds of a feather flock together" *exp.* "People who are similar attract each other."

> *usage example:* Scott's friends are all strange, but like they say, **birds of a feather flock together**.

> *translation:* Scott's friends are all strange, but like they say, people who are similar attract each other.

> **NOTE:** This expression may simply be shortened to: **birds of a feather** since the rest of the expression is merely inferred.

"Blood is thicker than water" *exp.* "Loyalty should be to the family first."

> *usage example:* Leon had a choice of moving to another city with his parents, or staying behind with his friends. Since **blood is thicker than water**, he decided to go with his family.

> *translation:* Leon had a choice of moving to another city with his parents, or staying behind with his friends. Since loyalty should be to the family first, he decided to go with his family.

"Close, but no cigar" *exp.* "Being partially accurate is still inaccurate."

> *usage example:* "Watch me shoot this target. I bet I hit it on my first try." **"Close, but no cigar**. Better luck next time."

> *translation:* "Watch me shoot this target. I bet I hit it on my first try." "Being partially accurate is still inaccurate. Better luck next time."

"Crime doesn't pay" *exp.* "Whatever the outcome, it's not worth the consequences of committing a crime."

usage example: Sheila stole a thousand dollars from work and now she's going to jail. It's the third time she's done that to an employer. When will she learn that **crime doesn't pay**?

translation: Sheila stole a thousand dollars from work and now she's going to jail. It's the third time she's done that to an employer. When will she learn that it's not worth the consequences of committing a crime?

"Curiosity killed the cat" *exp.* "People who are too inquisitive and meddlesome can get themselves into trouble."

usage example: "I think that there are some criminals who just moved into the apartment next door to mine. I'm going to go investigate."

"I wouldn't do that if I were you. They could be dangerous! After all, **curiosity killed the cat**!"

translation: "I think that there are some criminals who just moved into the apartment next door to mine. I'm going to go investigate."

"I wouldn't do that if I were you. They could be dangerous! After all, people who are too inquisitive and meddlesome can get themselves into trouble!"

"Don't count your chickens before they hatch" *exp.* "Don't assume success until it actually happens."

usage example: "My job interview went so well today that I'm going to quit my current job!"

"Now, wait! **Don't count your chickens before they hatch**!"

translation: "My job interview went so well today that I'm going to quit my current job!"

"Now, wait! Don't assume success until it actually happens!"

VARIATION (1): **Don't count your chickens before they've hatched** *exp.*

VARIATION (2): **Don't go counting your chickens before they hatch/ they're hatched** *exp.*

"Don't look a gift horse in the mouth" *exp.* "Don't criticize gifts that you receive."

usage example: "I wanted a red bicycle for my birthday. This one is green!"
"**Don't look a gift horse in the mouth**. You could have received nothing!"

translation: "I wanted a red bicycle for my birthday. This one is green!"
"Don't criticize the gifts that you receive. You could have received nothing!"

"Don't put all your eggs in one basket" *exp.* "Don't gamble your possibility of success on one goal since failure could mean losing everything."

usage example: "If I get this job, I can pay off my debts. Then I'll buy a car, new clothes, and move to a new apartment!"
"**Don't put all your eggs in one basket**. What if you don't get the job?

translation: "If I get this job, I can pay off my debts. Then I'll buy a car, new clothes, and move to a new apartment!"
"Don't gamble your possibility of success on one goal since failure could mean losing everything. What if you don't get the job?"

"Don't put the cart before the horse" *exp.* "Don't do things out of order."

usage example: You're going to buy a wedding ring before you ask Jan to marry you? **Don't put the cart before the horse!**

translation: You're going to buy a wedding ring before you ask Jan to marry you? Don't do things out of order!

"Early to bed, early to rise makes a man healthy, wealthy, and wise" *exp.* "People who go to bed early are healthier, wealthier, and wiser than people who go to bed late."

usage example: "You're going to bed already? It's only eight o'clock!"
"You know what they say. **Early to bed, early to rise makes a man healthy, wealthy, and wise**."

translation: "You're going to bed already? It's only eight o'clock!"
"You know what they say. People who go to bed early are healthier, wealthier, and wiser than people who go to bed late."

"Easy come, easy go" *exp.* "Anything that can be easily acquired, can be easily taken away."

usage example: I won a thousand dollars today playing roulette. Then I lost it all on a horse race. Oh, well. **Easy come, easy go**.

translation: I won a thousand dollars today playing roulette. Then I lost it all on a horse race. Oh, well. Anything that can be easily acquired, can be easily taken away.

"Every [gray] cloud has a silver lining" *exp.* "Bad events are always followed by good events."

usage example: Remember how upset you were last week because you didn't get the job you wanted? Now today, you were offered a job that pays twice as much! **Every [gray] cloud has a silver lining**.

translation: Remember how upset you were last week because you didn't get the job you wanted? Now today, you were offered a job that pays twice as much! Bad events are always followed by good events.

VARIATION: **Behind every [gray] cloud is a silver lining** *exp.*

"Every dog has its/his day" *exp.* "Every person will have his/her moment of glory."

usage example: I just won a thousand dollars! I guess it's true when they say that **every dog has its/his day**!

translation: I just won a thousand dollars! I guess it's true when they say that every person will have his/her moment of glory!

"Familiarity breeds contempt" *exp.* "Getting to know someone very well could be dangerous since you may notice unacceptable qualities."

usage example: We were such good friends until we started living together. I guess it's true when they say that **familiarity breeds contempt**.

translation: We were such good friends until we started living together. I guess it's true when they say that getting to know someone very well could be dangerous since you may notice unacceptable qualities.

"Finders-keepers, losers-weepers" *exp.* (used primarily among children) "If you find something, you're allowed to keep it even though the person who lost it may cry."

usage example: "Hey, you have my pen! I dropped it here by accident!"
"It's mine now. **Finders-keepers, losers-weepers**!"

translation: "Hey, you have my pen! I dropped it here by accident!"
"It's mine now. If you find something, you're allowed to keep it."

"Haste makes waste" *exp.* "If you do something in a hurry, you'll ruin it (and you'll probably have to do it over)."

> *usage example:* I know you want to leave early, but take your time with these calculations. Remember, **haste makes waste**.

> *translation:* I know you want to leave early, but take your time with these calculations. Remember, if you do the job in a hurry, you'll make mistakes.

"He who laughs last, laughs longest" *exp.* "You did something bad to me, but now I'm going to do something even worse to you."

> *usage example:* Steve kept laughing about the trick he played on me. But I told him that he'd better stop laughing because **he who laughs last, laughs longest**.

> *translation:* Steve kept laughing about the trick he played on me. But I told him that he'd better stop laughing because I'm going to do something worse to him.

> **VARIATION:** **"He who laughs last, laughs best"** *exp.*

"Honesty is the best policy" *exp.* "You'll always get the best results if you're honest."

> *usage example:* You'd better confess the truth to your mother. **Honesty is the best policy**.

> *translation:* You'd better confess the truth to your mother. You'll always get the best results if you're honest.

"If at first you don't succeed, try, try again" *exp.* "If you don't succeed in doing something the first time, keep on trying."

> *usage example:* What do you mean you're ready to give up? **If at first you don't succeed, try, try again**.

translation: What do you mean you're ready to give up? If you don't succeed in doing something the first time, keep on trying.

"It takes two to tango" *exp.* "It takes two people to do certain activities."

usage example: What do you mean the fight was my fault? **It takes two to tango**!

translation: What do you mean the fight was my fault? It takes two people to have a fight!

"Live and let live" *exp.* "Live your own life without telling others how to live theirs."

usage example: Why do you care how my friends live their lives. It's none of your business. **Live and let live**.

translation: Why do you care how my friends live their lives. It's none of your business. Live your own life without telling others how to live theirs.

"Money is the root of all evil" *exp.* "Money causes all the problems in the world."

usage example: A lot of people will do anything for money even if it hurts others. I think it's true when people say that **money is the root of all evil**.

translation: A lot of people will do anything for money even if it hurts others. I think it's true when people say that money causes all of the problems in the world.

"Necessity is the mother of invention" *exp.* "If you're desperate enough, you'll find a way to accomplish anything."

usage example: I couldn't afford to take my car to the mechanic so, I figured out a way to fix my car for free. **Necessity is the mother of invention**.

translation: I couldn't afford to take my car to the mechanic so, I figured out a way to fix my car for free. If you're desperate enough, you'll find a way to accomplish anything.

"No news is good news" *exp.* "If you haven't received any news, assume it's good news."

usage example: I went to my doctor the other day for some medical tests and I haven't heard from him. I shouldn't worry. After all, **no news is good news**.

translation: I went to my doctor the other day for some medical tests and I haven't heard from him. I shouldn't worry. After all, if you haven't received any news, assume it's good news.

"Nothing ventured, nothing gained" *exp.* "If you don't attempt something difficult, you'll never benefit from the potential rewards."

usage example: I know you're nervous to ask the boss for a raise, but remember, **nothing ventured, nothing gained**.

translation: I know you're nervous to ask the boss for a raise, but remember, if you don't attempt it, you'll never get anything.

"One good turn deserves another" *exp.* "A good deed should be rewarded with another good deed."

usage example: I really appreciate you helping me move yesterday. Since **one good turn deserves another**, I'd like to give you these free airplane tickets to Europe.

translation: I really appreciate you helping me move yesterday. Since one good deed should be rewarded with another, I'd like to give you these free airplane tickets to Europe.

"One's bark is worse than one's bite" *exp.* said of someone who is threatening but not dangerous.

usage example: Our new boss yells a lot but don't worry. **His bark is worse than his bite**.

translation: Our new boss yells a lot but don't worry. He's threatening but not dangerous.

"Practice makes perfect" *exp.* "You can only perfect your skills by practicing."

usage example: You need to play the piano at least an hour every day. **Practice makes perfect**.

translation: You need to play the piano at least an hour every day. You can only perfect your skills by practicing.

"Practice what you preach" *exp.* "Take the same advice you give others."

usage example: You always tell me how terrible it is for people to lie, but today you lied to me! Why don't you **practice what you preach**!

translation: You always tell me how terrible it is for people to lie, but today you lied to me! Why don't you take the same advice you give others!

"Seeing is believing" *exp.* "I'll believe it when I see it."

usage example: I didn't believe you were an acrobat but **seeing is believing**!

translation: I didn't believe you were an acrobat but now that I've seen you perform, I believe it!

"The early bird gets the worm" *exp.* "The person who begins his/her work the earliest gets all the opportunities and the most accomplished."

usage example: I like to get to work before anyone else. **The early bird gets the worm**.

translation: I like to get to work before anyone else. The person who begins his/her work the earliest gets the most accomplished.

VARIATION: **The early bird catches the worm** *exp.*

"The more the merrier" *exp.* "The more people involved in a particular activity, the more fun it will be."

    usage example: Why don't you join us on our picnic today? **The more the merrier!**

    translation: Why don't you join us on our picnic today? The more people involved, the more fun it will be!

"There are plenty of other fish in the sea" *exp.* "There are many other opportunities in the world."

    usage example: He's always so mean to you. Why don't you go find someone else? **There are plenty of other fish in the sea.**

    translation: He's always so mean to you. Why don't you go find someone else? There are many other opportunities for you to meet someone.

"There's more than one way to skin a cat" *exp.* "There are many ways to achieve one's goal;" "There are lots of right ways to do something."

    usage example: If you can't resolve your problem the first time, try another way. Remember, **there's more than one way to skin a cat.**

    translation: If you can't resolve your problem the first time, try another way. Remember, there are many ways to achieve one's goal.

"To kill two birds with one stone" *exp.* "To accomplish two goals in one deed."

usage example: I have to take my sister to the airport by 2:00pm and pick up a friend at 3:00pm. This will be easy. I'll be able **to kill two birds with one stone**.

translation: I have to take my sister to the airport by 2:00pm and pick up a friend at 3:00pm. This will be easy. I'll be able to accomplish two goals at the same time.

"Variety is the spice of life" *exp.* "People's differences make the world interesting."

usage example: My new roommate and I are so different. I hope we don't have any problems living together. I just have to remember that **variety is the spice of life**.

translation: My new roommate and I are so different. I hope we don't have any problems living together. I just have to remember that people's differences make the world interesting.

"We'll cross that bridge when we come to it" *exp.* "We'll face that problem when it arises."

usage example: "I'm so nervous about my singing audition. What'll I do if they ask me to sing something I don't know?" **"You'll cross that bridge when you come to it."**

translation: "I'm so nervous about my singing audition. What'll I do if they ask me to sing something I don't know?" "You'll face that problem when it arises."

VARIATION: **"We'll cross that bridge when we get to it"** *exp.*

"When the cat's away, the mice will play" *exp.* "When the authorities are gone, mischief begins."

usage example: As soon as we left the house, our children invited their friends over for a wild party. **When the cat's away, the mice will play**.

translation: As soon as we left the house, our children invited their friends over for a wild party. When the authorities are gone, mischief begins.

"Where there's a will, there's a way" *exp.* "If something is desired enough, a means will be found to achieve it."

usage example: "How will I ever get enough money to go to Hawaii for the summer?"
"Where there's a will, there's a way."

translation: "How will I ever get enough money to go to Hawaii for the summer?"
"If you want it badly enough, you'll find a way."

"You can't judge a book by its cover" *exp.* "You can't judge something by how it looks on the outside."

usage example: I thought Beth was so nice at first. She looked so sweet and friendly. Then I discovered she's actually insensitive, mean, and jealous. One thing's for sure. **You can't judge a book by its cover**.

translation: I thought Beth was so nice at first. She looked so sweet and friendly. Then I discovered she's actually insensitive, mean, and jealous. One thing's for sure. You can't judge something by how it looks from the outside.

"You can't teach an old dog new tricks" *exp.* "Old people can't learn new skills;" "It's difficult to break an old pattern of behavior."

usage example: I'm seventy years old and I'm never going to be able to learn to use a computer. I'm afraid **you can't teach an old dog new tricks**.

translation: I'm seventy years old and I'm never going to be able to learn to use a computer. I'm afraid you can't teach old people new skills.

Lesson Fourteen - SURVIVAL IDIOMS & PHRASES

Dialogue In Slang

"Freeze!"

DIALOGUE

Donna is writing a letter to her friend, Lucy.

Dear Lucy:

You won't believe what happened yesterday. I was **held up**! First I heard someone yell "**Freeze!**"so I stopped. Then a man's voice from behind me said "**Shut up** and **hand over your wallet**." I didn't want to make him mad so I did exactly what he wanted. Then all of a sudden, I heard a cop yell, "**We've got you covered**. Drop the weapon." At first, the robber didn't respond. Then the **cops** approached him and ordered him to lean against his car and "**spread 'em**." Then they **cuffed** him, read him his **Mirandas**, and **took him in**. They probably **booked him** and threw him in jail. What a day!

Lesson Fourteen - SURVIVAL IDIOMS & PHRASES

Translation of dialogue in standard English

DIALOGUE

Donna is writing a letter to her friend, Lucy.

Dear Lucy:

You won't believe what happened yesterday. I was **robbed**! First I heard someone yell "**Don't move**!"so I stopped. Then a man's voice from behind me said "**Stop talking** and **give me your wallet**." I didn't want to make him mad so I did exactly what he wanted. Then all of a sudden, I heard a **police officer** yell, "**We're aiming our guns at you**. Drop the weapon." At first, the robber didn't respond. Then the **police officers** approached him and ordered him to lean against his car and "**spread his arms and legs apart**." Then they **put handcuffs on** him, read him his **constitutional rights**, and **took him to the police station**. They probably **registered him as a suspect** and threw him in jail. What a day!

Lesson Fourteen - SURVIVAL IDIOMS & PHRASES

Dialogue in slang as it would be heard

"Freeze!"

DIALOGUE

Donna'z wriding a ledder to 'er friend, Lucy.

Dear Lucy:

You won't b'lieve what happened yesterday. I was **held up**! First I heard someone yell "**Freeze**!"so I stopped. Then a man's voice fr'm b'hin' me said "**Shud up** 'n **hand over yer wallet**." I didn' wanna make 'im mad so I did exactly whad 'e wan'ed. Then all of a sudden, I heard a **cop** yell, "**We've got chew covered**. Drop the weapon." At first, the robber didn't respond. Then the **cops** approached 'im 'n ordered 'im ta lean against 'is car 'n "**spread 'em**." Then they **cuffed** 'im, read 'im 'is **Mirandas**, and **took 'im in**. They prob'ly **booked 'im** 'n threw 'im in jail. Whad a day!

Vocabulary

book someone (to) *exp.* to register someone as a suspect at the police station.

> *usage example:* John was **booked** on suspicion of murder.
>
> *translation:* John was registered at the police station on suspicion of murder.

cop *n.* police officer.

> *usage example:* You're driving too fast and there's a **cop** behind you!
>
> *translation:* You're driving too fast and there's a police officer behind you!
>
> **NOTE (1):** This is an abbreviation of the slang term *"copper,"* used only in old gangster movies and in jest, due to the copper buttons worn by police officers.
>
> **NOTE (2):** This is a popular slang term even among police officers.

cover someone (to) *exp.* **1.** to aim a gun at someone • **2.** to protect someone by using a gun.

> *usage example (1):* Surrender. **We've got you covered**!
>
> *translation:* Surrender. We're aiming our guns at you.
>
> *usage example (2):* I think the criminals are in that room. I'll **cover you** as you move in.
>
> *translation:* I think the criminals are in that room. I'll protect you with my gun as your walk in.
>
> **NOTE:** The difference between definitions **1.** and **2.** depends on the context.

*Don't move! I've got you **covered**.*

cuff someone (to) *exp.* to put handcuffs on someone.

    usage example: **Cuff 'im.**

        translation: Put handcuffs on him.

           NOTE: "*'Im*" is a common reduction for "him."

freeze (to) *interj.* to stop and hold completely still.

    usage example: **Freeze** or I'll shoot!

        translation: Stop and hold completely still or I'll shoot!

"Give 'im 'iz Mirandas" *exp.* "Give him his Miranda rights."

NOTE (1):   "*'Iz*" is a common reduction for "his."

VARIATION (1):   **"Read 'im 'iz Mirandas"** *exp.*

VARIATION (2):   **"Mirandize 'im"** *exp.*

VARIATION (3):   **"Read 'im 'iz rights"**

NOTE (2):   *"Miranda rights"* originated from a court case where a suspect (with the last name of Miranda) incriminated himself. Since forcing a suspect to incriminate him/herself is a violation of constitutional rights, the judge in this case declared that any suspect must be read his/her constitutional rights before questioning can be started. These rights are called the *"Miranda rights"* or *"Mirandas."*

The Miranda rights are as follows:

You have the right to remain silent. If you give up the right to remain silent, anything you say can and will be used against you in a court of law. You have the right to speak with an attorney and to have an attorney present during questioning. If you so desire and cannot afford one, an attorney will be appointed for you without charge before questioning.
• *Do you understand each of these rights that I have explained to you?*
• *Do you wish to give up your right to remain silent?*
• *Do you wish to give up your right to speak to an attorney and have him present during questioning?*

hand over something (to) *exp.* to surrender something (to someone).

usage example: **Hand over** your wallet!

translation: Surrender your wallet!

VARIATION: **to hand something over** *exp.*

usage example: **Hand it over**!

translation: Surrender it (to me)!

hold someone up (to) *exp.* to rob someone.

    usage example: I got **held up** today in front of my house!

      translation: I got robbed today in front of my house!

      ALSO: **to hold someone up at gunpoint** *exp.* to rob someone by using a gun.

shut up (to) *interj.* to stop talking.

    usage example: If you don't **shut up**, I'll kill you!

      translation: If you don't stop talking, I'll kill you!

      NOTE: The expression *"Shut up!"* is considered rather coarse. The polite form would be *"Please be quiet."*

spread them (to) *exp.* to spread apart one's arms and legs.

    usage example: Lie on the ground and **spread 'em**!

      translation: Lie on the ground and spread your arms and legs apart!

      NOTE: In this expression, *"'em"* refers to "them" meaning "the arms and legs."

take someone in (to) *exp.* to take someone to the police station for processing.

    usage example: Let's **take 'im in**.

      translation: Let's take him to the police station and process him.

Practice The Vocabulary ▦

(Answers to Lesson 14, p. 273)

A. CROSSWORD
Fill in the crossword puzzle on the opposite page by choosing the correct word(s) from the list below.

book

covered

cuffed

freeze

hand over

held

Mirandas

shut

spread

took him in

Across

3. The officer arrested the suspect and _____ . They should arrive at the police station in a few minutes.

16. Don't worry. I'll protect you. I've got you _____ .

24. Stop!

29. She talks all the time. Doesn't she ever _____ up?

30. _____ 'em! Your arms and legs aren't far enough apart!

Down

7. _____ your wallet. I said give it to me now!

9. Before an officer can arrest a suspect, the officer must read him his _____ .

13. I'm taking you to the police station to _____ you on suspicion of murder.

23. I was _____ up yesterday and was forced to surrender my purse!

26. The officer told the suspect to put his hands behind his back. Then the officer _____ him.

CROSSWORD PUZZLE

B. Choose the correct phrase that best fits the idiom.

1. The police officer read the suspect his **Mirandas**.
   - ☐ a. Then the officer put him to bed.
   - ☐ b. Then the officer let him go.
   - ☐ c. Then the officer took him to the police station.

2. I got **held up** today by a man with a gun!
   - ☐ a. I must have been in the air for five minutes!
   - ☐ b. Then it was my turn to lift *him* up.
   - ☐ c. He took all my money.

3. The officer arrested the suspect and **took him in**.
   - ☐ a. I guess he'll be spending the night in jail.
   - ☐ b. I guess the officer lost him accidentally.
   - ☐ c. They must have gone back to the officer's house.

4. Come out! We've got you **covered**!
   - ☐ a. We're all aiming our guns at you.
   - ☐ b. We have a nice warm blanket here for you.
   - ☐ c. We don't have any guns.

5. **Hand over** your money!
   - ☐ a. Don't give it to me!
   - ☐ b. Give it to me, now!
   - ☐ c. Give it to someone else!

6. **Shut up**!
   - ☐ a. I said to keep talking!
   - ☐ b. Why are you always so quiet?
   - ☐ c. Don't you ever stop talking?

7. The officer **cuffed** the suspect.
   - ☐ a. That way the suspect won't be able to use his arms.
   - ☐ b. That way the suspect can use his arms easier.
   - ☐ c. Then the officer rolled up his own sleeves.

8. **Freeze**!
   - ☐ a. Keep moving!
   - ☐ b. It's getting cold in here.
   - ☐ c. Stop everything you're doing!

C. Underline the word that best completes the phrase.

1. (**Sneeze**, **Freeze**, **Please**) or I'll shoot!

2. Yesterday Bob was (**looked**, **booked**, **cooked**) for murder. His family had no idea that he was a killer.

3. Shut (**up**, **down**, **over**)! If you say one more word, I'm going to shoot you!

4. Lie on the ground and (**spread**, **thread**, **bread**) 'em!

5. The officer (**cuffed**, **puffed**, **huffed**) the suspect. The officer wanted to make sure that the suspect kept his arms behind his back.

6. (**Hand**, **Foot**, **Elbow**) over your wallet!

7. I was held (**up**, **down**, **in**) today! All my money was stolen!

8. Don't move. We've got you (**smothered**, **buttered**, **covered**).

9. Before a suspect can be arrested, the officer must read him his (**Pandas**, **Verandas**, **Mirandas**).

10. You're under arrest. I'm taking you (**out**, **over**, **in**).

E. DICTATION ▣
Test Your Oral Comprehension
(This dictation can be found in Appendix A on page 282).

If you are following along with your cassette, you will now hear a paragraph containing many of the idioms from this section. The paragraph will be read by a native speaker at normal conversational speed (which may seem fast to you at first). In addition, the words will be pronounced *as you would actually hear them in a conversation,* including many common reductions.

The first time the paragraph is presented, simply listen in order to get accustomed to the speed and heavy use of reductions. The paragraph will then be read again with a pause after each group of words to give you time to write down what you heard. The third time the paragraph is read, follow along with what you have written.

A CLOSER LOOK:
Survival Words & Phrases
(That Could Save Your Life!)

Unfortunately, crime is a part of any big city. Being a victim of a crime is certainly horrifying for anyone. However, as a non-native speaker, you are at an unquestionable disadvantage. The reason is simple. In order for a criminal to commit a crime, he must act quickly or risk getting caught. If you slow him down in any way (such as not understanding him and asking him to repeat himself), he could get angry and become unpredictable.

For your own safety, **_your goal is to understand his demands immediately_** and give him what he wants. Hopefully, this will encourage him to leave quickly.

Even being stopped by a police officer can be rather intimidating and scary, especially if you don't understand his/her questions.

Following are some common words and expressions that you may hear used by criminals and police officers. You may already understand many of these

phrases if you were to see them written. However, when you hear them spoken, you may not understand them at all. Why? Simple. Native- born Americans constantly use reductions which are abbreviated forms of a particular word. (The third dialogue page of each chapter has been written using popular reductions.) For example: "want to" becomes *"wanna;"* "going to" becomes *"gonna;"* etc.
(For a complete list of reductions and contractions, see **STREET TALK -1** *p. 13, Commonly Used Contractions.*)

As you've already seen in the previous dialogues, these reductions will definitely change the way words are pronounced, making it difficult to understand them. It is important that you learn the following phrases using reductions since this is how you will undoubtedly hear them.

NOTE: The following phrases and expression are divided into two groups:
1) Phrases Used by Criminals; and **2)** Phrases Used by Police Officers. Please note that many phrases can be used by both groups and will therefore appear twice.

In addition, the terms and expressions that were presented in the vocabulary section will be found here as well. This was done in an effort to keep the most commonly used phrases together for easy reference.

PHRASES USED BY CRIMINALS

blow someone away (to) *exp.* to shoot someone.
> *usage example:* One move and I'll **blow you away**!
>
> *translation:* One move and I'll shoot you!

carjack (to) *v.* to steal a car directly from the owner by use of force.
> *usage example:* I just got **carjacked**!
>
> *translation:* I just got my car stolen by someone carrying a weapon!
>
> **ALSO:** **carjacking** *n.* the act of stealing a car directly from the owner by use of force.

false move *exp.* an incorrect maneuver.

> *usage example:* One **false move** and I'll kill you.

> *translation:* One incorrect maneuver and I'll kill you.

"Freeze!" *interj.* "Don't move!"

> **NOTE:** This expression is also used by police officers.

"Gimme your money/wallet/etc." *exp.* "Give me your money/wallet/etc."

> **NOTE:** *"Gimme"* is a common reduction of "give me."

hand over something (to) *exp.* to surrender something (to someone).

> *usage example:* **Hand over** your wallet!

> *translation:* Surrender your wallet!

> **VARIATION:** **to hand something over** *exp.*

> > *usage example:* **Hand** your wallet **over**!

> > *translation:* Surrender your wallet!

"Hit the dirt!" *exp.* "Get down on the ground!"

> **VARIATION:** "**Hit the ground!**" *exp.*

> **NOTE:** This expression may also be used by police officers.

hold someone up (to) *exp.* to rob someone.

> *usage example:* I got **held up** in broad daylight!

> *translation:* I got robbed in the middle of the day!

> **NOTE:** The expression *"in broad daylight"* is commonly used when talking about crimes committed in the middle of the day.

> **ALSO:** **to hold someone up at gunpoint** *exp.* to rob someone by using a gun.

hold-up *exp.* robbery.

> *usage example:* This is a **hold-up**. Don't anyone move!

> *translation:* This is a robbery. Don't anyone move!

NOTE (1): This expression was originated since victims are made to *"hold up"* their arms during a robbery to show that they are not carrying weapons.

SYNONYM: SEE: **stick up** *exp.*

ALSO: SEE: **to hold someone up** *exp.*

"I'll blow your head off!" *exp.* "I'll shoot you in the head!"

usage example: Don't move or **I'll blow your head off**!

translation: Don't move or I'll shoot you in the head!

"Keep yer hands where I c'n see 'em" *exp.*

NOTE (1): *"Yer"* is a common reduction of "your."

NOTE (2): *"C'n"* is a common reduction of "can."

NOTE (3): *"'Em"* is a common reduction of "them."

NOTE (4): This expression may also be used by police officers.

let someone have it (to) *exp.* to kill someone (either figuratively or literally, depending on the context).

usage example: If you don't gimme yer money right now, I'm gonna **let cha have it**!

translation: If you don't give me your money right now, I'm going to kill you!

NOTE: *"Let cha"* and *"let chew"* are a common reductions of "let you."

"Put 'em up!" *exp.* "Put them up!"

NOTE (1): In this expression, *'em* (short for "them") refers to "the hands."

NOTE (2): This expression may also be used by police officers.

VARIATION: **"Stick 'em up!"** *exp.*

SEE: **stick up** *exp.*

"Shut up!" *interj.* "Stop talking!"

usage example: **Shut up** or I'll shoot!

translation: Stop talking or I'll shoot!

NOTE: This expression may also be used by police officers.

"Stay down!" *exp.* "Stay on the ground!"

stick-up *exp.* robbery.

usage example: Did you hear about the **stick up** at the bank today?

translation: Did you hear about the robbery at the bank today?

NOTE: This expression was originated since victims are made to *"stick up"* their arms during a robbery to show that they are not carrying weapons.

waste someone (to) *exp.* to kill someone.

usage example: If you don't hand over your money right now, I'm gonna **waste** you!

translation: If you don't surrender your money right now, I'm going to kill you!

NOTE: *"Gonna"* is a common reduction for "going to."

PHRASES USED BY POLICE OFFICERS

broad daylight (in) *exp.* a common expression used when referring to a crime committed in the middle of the day.

usage example: The bank was robbed in **broad daylight**.

translation: The bank was robbed in the middle of the day.

cuff someone (to) *exp.* to put handcuffs on someone.

usage example: **Cuff 'im!**

translation: Put handcuffs on him!

NOTE: *"'Im"* is a common reduction for "him."

D.U.I. *exp.* a citation for Driving Under the Influence (of alcohol).

usage example: I'm issuing you a **D.U.I.**

translation: I'm issuing you a citation for **d**riving **u**nder the **i**nfluence of alcohol.

VARIATION: **D.W.I.** *exp.* a citation for **d**riving **w**hile **i**ntoxicated.

"Freeze!" *interj.* "Don't move!"

NOTE: This expression may also be used by criminals.

frisk someone (to) *exp.* to search someone's clothing for hidden or illegal possessions.

usage example: The police officer **frisked** the man for drugs.

translation: The police officer searched the man for hidden drugs.

"Give 'im 'iz Mirandas" *exp.* "Give him his Miranda rights."

NOTE (1): "'*Iz*" is a common reduction for "his."

VARIATION (1): **"Read 'im 'iz Mirandas"** *exp.*

VARIATION (2): **"Mirandize 'im"** *exp.*

VARIATION (3): **"Read 'im 'iz rights"** *exp.*

"Hands b'hin' d'jer head / back!" *exp.* "Hands behind your head back!"

NOTE (1): "*B'hin'*" is a common reduction for "behind". In the example above, the native-born speaker will either say "*b'hin' d'jer*" or "*b'hind yer*" at his/her discretion.

NOTE (2): "*D'jer*" is a common reduction for "your" when preceded by the letter "D." For example: *I think you dropped your keys behin'* **d'jer** (or **behind yer**) *car.*

NOTE (3): "*T'cher*" is a common reduction for "your" when preceded by the letter "T." For example: *Put* **t'cher** *sweater in the closet.*

NOTE (4): "*Yer*" is a common reduction for "your" when preceded by any letter. For example: *Where's* **yer** *sister today?* • *Is that* **yer** (or **t'cher**) *watch?*

It is important to note that *"yer"* and *"y'r"* can always be used as a reduction for "your" or "you're." However, when preceded by the letter "D" or "T" (as previously demonstrated), the speaker has the choice of an additional reduction.

"Hit the dirt!" *exp.* "Get down on the ground!"
VARIATION: "Hit the ground!" *exp.*

NOTE: This expression may also be used by criminals.

"Keep yer hands where I c'n see 'em" *exp.*
NOTE (1): *"Yer"* is a common reduction of "your."

NOTE (2): *"C'n"* is a common reduction of "can."

NOTE (3): *"'Em"* is a common reduction of "them."

NOTE (4): This expression may also be used by criminals.

"Lemme see yer hands" *exp.* "Let me see your hands."
NOTE (1): *"Lemme"* is a common reduction for "let me."

NOTE (2): *"Yer"* is a common reduction for "your."

"Let's take 'im in 'n book 'im" *exp.* "Let's take him into the police station and register him."
NOTE: **to book someone** *exp.* to register someone as a suspect by putting his/her name into a logbook at the police station.

"On your knees!" *exp.* "Get on your knees!"

"Put 'em up!" *exp.* "Put them up!"
NOTE (1): In this expression, *"'em"* (short for "them") refers to "your hands."

NOTE (2): This expression may also be used by criminals.

VARIATION: "Stick 'em up!" *exp.*

SEE: **stick up** *exp.*

"Shut up!" *interj.* "Stop talking!"

   usage example: **Shut up** or I'll shoot!

    translation: Stop talking or I'll shoot!

     NOTE: This expression may also be used by criminals.

"Spread 'em!" *exp.* "Spread your arms and legs apart!"

   NOTE: In this expression, *"'em"* refers to "them" meaning "the arms and legs."

"Step oudda the vehicle" *exp.* "Get out of the car."

   NOTE: *"Outta"* (pronounced *"oudda"*) is a common reduction of "out of."

suspect *n.* one who is under suspicion of having committed a crime.

   usage example: You are our prime **suspect**.

    translation: You are the person that we most suspect of having committed the crime.

"We've got you covered" *exp.* "We're aiming our guns at you."

   usage example: Surrender. **We've got you covered**!

    translation: Surrender. We're aiming our guns at you.

     NOTE: **to cover someone** *exp.* **1.** to aim a gun at someone • **2.** to protect someone by using a gun.

      usage example (1): Surrender. **We've got you covered**!

       translation: Surrender. We're aiming our guns at you!

      usage example (2): I think the criminals are in that room. I'll **cover you** as you go in.

       translation: I think the criminals are in that room. I'll protect you with my gun as you go in.

     NOTE: The difference between definitions **1.** and **2.** depends on the context.

REVIEW EXAM FOR LESSONS 11-14

(Answers to Review, p. 274)

A. Underline the appropriate words that best complete the phrase.

1. I feel great. I'm in (**tip-top, pitter-patter, mish-mash**) shape.

2. I don't trust him. I don't think he's on the (**vim-and-vigor, out-and-out, up-and-up**).

3. We haven't spoken in two years but today we decided to let (**through-and-through, bygones be bygones, R-and-R**).

4. She actually likes that painting? One thing's for sure. There's no accounting for (**smell, touch, taste**).

5. Look at all these letters I received today! When it rains, it (**rains, pours, snows**).

6. I got held (**down, in, up**) yesterday. The robber took all my money!

7. Officer, here's your murder suspect. (**Book, Magazine, Newspaper**) 'im!

8. I'm exhausted. I think I need some (**M-and-M, A-and-A, R-and-R**).

B. CROSSWORD
Step 1: Fill in the blanks with the appropriate word(s) from the list below.
Step 2: Using your answers, fill in the crossword puzzle on page 255.

eye	mind	toe-to-toe
freeze	pours	up-and-up
hand it over	shut up	words
knack	span	
mile	top	

Across

16. I bought you a present while I was on vacation. It's just a little knick- _____ I thought you'd like.

19. Don't tell me how much you like me. Show me. Actions speak louder than _____ .

24. Give it to me. I said to _____ !

33. I've been cleaning my house all day. It's finally spic-and- _____ .

37. _____ or I'll shoot!

45. Bonnie always takes advantage of people. Give her an inch, she'll take a _____ .

Down

3. Ever since Michelle moved away, she never writes to me. Out of sight, out of _____ .

7. Don't trust him. He's not on the _____ .

15. I'm in tip- _____ condition. I've never felt better!

18. Steve has been going _____ with everyone in the office today. I've never seen him so disagreeable!

20. Helen talks so much! I wish she'd just _____ .

22. Look at all these gifts I received! When it rains, it _____ .

38. Ed and I don't see eye-to-_____ on most issues.

CROSSWORD PUZZLE

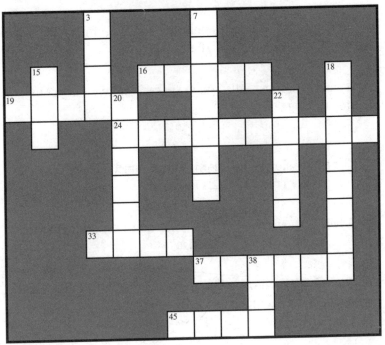

C. TRUE or FALSE
Are the following sentences (containing idiomatic expressions) true or false?

1. If you're in **tip-top** shape, you're in bad health.
   ☐ True   ☐ False

2. If your house is **spic-and-span**, it's very dirty.
   ☐ True   ☐ False

3. When someone is on the **up-and-up**, he/she is trustworthy.
   ☐ True   ☐ False

4. If you see **eye-to-eye** with your friend, you are in agreement.
   ☐ True   ☐ False

5. When someone tells you to **freeze**, you shouldn't move.
   ☐ True   ☐ False

6. When you **hand over** something, you are refusing to let it go.
   ☐ True   ☐ False

7. If a police officer tells you to **spread 'em**, you are being told to stop talking.
   ☐ True   ☐ False

8. The expression **out of sight, out of mind** means "fantastic."
   ☐ True   ☐ False

9. When a situation is reversed, **the shoe's on the other foot**.
   ☐ True   ☐ False

10. If you **let bygones be bygones**, you are choosing to forget the negative events that happened in the past.
    ☐ True   ☐ False

D. CONTEXT EXERCISE.
Choose the best idiom from the right column that goes with the phrase in the left column.

☐ 1. Stephanie always tells me that if I ever need her help, she'll be there but she never is!

☐ 2. How can Tracy wear that ugly dress?

☐ 3. When I visited Japan, I was asked to take off my shoes before I entered the house.

☐ 4. Catch that man!

☐ 5. Doesn't she ever stop talking?

☐ 6. Every day, people are moving out of the city.

☐ 7. The boss wants to talk with Joe about his work.

☐ 8. I like several types of music: classical, rock and roll, hard rock, and punk.

☐ 9. Do you have children?

☐ 10. Is your house always this clean?

A. I think I hear the **pitter-patter** of little feet.

B. I guess **there's no accounting for taste**.

C. I think this is going to be a serious **tête-à-tête**.

D. **When in Rome, do as the Romans**.

E. It's happening **more and more**.

F. I have a real **mish-mash** of different tastes.

G. I wish mine could be this **spic-and-span**.

H. He just **held me up**!

I. I wish she'd just **shut up**.

J. I finally told her that **actions speak louder than words**.

ANSWERS TO LESSONS 1-14

LESSON ONE - *I'm sure they'll "give you a fair shake"*

Practice the Vocabulary

A. 1. b
  2. c
  3. a
  4. b

  5. c
  6. a
  7. b
  8. c

B. 1. H
  2. E
  3. G
  4. C

  5. F
  6. B
  7. A
  8. D

C. **CROSSWORD**

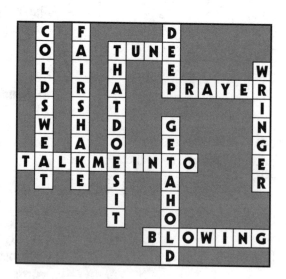

D. 1. get a hold of yourself
    2. go off the deep end
    3. [all] out of proportion
    4. fair shake
    5. talk me into
    6. that does it
    7. put through a wringer
    8. prayer

LESSON TWO - *"It's as plain as the nose on your face"*

Practice the Vocabulary

A. 1. incorrect
    2. incorrect
    3. correct
    4. correct
    5. incorrect
    6. correct
    7. incorrect
    8. incorrect

B. 1. a flash in the pan
    2. going together
    3. to pop the question
    4. love at first sight
    5. robbing the cradle
    6. as plain as the nose on your face
    7. to tie the knot
    8. you're pulling my leg
    9. hit the nail on the head
    10. to walk arm in arm

C. 1. head
    2. robbing
    3. nose
    4. pop
    5. leg
    6. pan
    7. first
    8. tie

D. 1. b
    2. c
    3. a
    4. a
    5. a
    6. b
    7. c
    8. b

LESSON THREE - *I think John's "getting cold feet"*

Practice the Vocabulary

A. 1. b   6. a
   2. c   7. c
   3. a   8. b
   4. b   9. a
   5. c   10. a

B. 1. come clean   5. cold feet
   2. on second thought   6. head on his shoulders
   3. if worse comes to worst   7. off the hook
   4. to fly off the handle;   8. break the news
      face the music   9. to fork over

C. 1. on second thought   5. face the music
   2. came clean   6. let you off the hook
   3. if worse comes to worst   7. break the news
   4. I've got cold feet   8. to fork over

D. 1. worst   6. handle
   2. break   7. fork
   3. feet   8. shoulders
   4. clean   9. hook
   5. music   10. thought

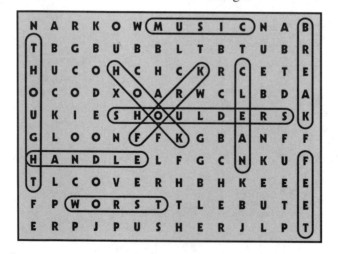

LESSON FOUR - *"Bite your tongue!"*

Practice the Vocabulary

A. **CROSSWORD**

B. 1. a   5. a
    2. c   6. c
    3. b   7. a
    4. c   8. a

C. 1. the time of my life   5. end of my rope
    2. hitch   6. hang in there
    3. sleep a wink   7. Bite your tongue
    4. like a log

D. 1. B   6. A
    2. D   7. E
    3. G   8. I
    4. C   9. J
    5. F   10. H

LESSON FIVE - *My house guest is "eating me out of house and home!"*

Practice the Vocabulary

A. 1. correct
   2. incorrect
   3. incorrect
   4. correct
   5. incorrect
   6. correct
   7. correct
   8. correct

B. 1. ear
   2. beating
   3. head
   4. straw
   5. home
   6. home
   7. posted
   8. gets

C. 1. a
   2. c
   3. a
   4. b
   5. c
   6. b
   7. a
   8. b
   9. a
   10. c

D. 1. a
   2. a
   3. a
   4. b
   5. a
   6. a
   7. b
   8. a

REVIEW EXAM FOR LESSONS 1-5

Practice the Vocabulary

A. 1. life
    2. head
    3. nose
    4. break
    5. worst

    6. leg
    7. pan
    8. arm
    9. cold
    10. blowing

B. **CROSSWORD**

C. 1. False
    2. True
    3. False
    4. False
    5. True

    6. True
    7. False
    8. False
    9. False
    10. True

D. 1. I
    2. A
    3. H
    4. D
    5. C

    6. E
    7. B
    8. G
    9. F
    10. J

LESSON SIX - *"A bad hair day"*

Practice the Vocabulary

A. 1. incorrect
   2. incorrect
   3. correct
   4. correct

   5. incorrect
   6. correct
   7. correct
   8. incorrect

B. 1. a bad hair day
   2. to go to town
   3. behind my back
   4. all dolled up
   5. getting on your nerves

   6. fishing for compliments
   7. making cracks about him/her
   8. no-host
   9. buying into it
   10. getting on your case

C. 1. fishing
   2. town
   3. nerves
   4. back
   5. up

   6. buy
   7. day
   8. case
   9. no
   10. cracks

D. 1. b
   2. c
   3. a
   4. b

   5. a
   6. c
   7. b
   8. a

LESSON SEVEN - *Jodi is "getting the hang of" skiing*

Practice the Vocabulary

A. **CROSSWORD**

```
            B I T E T H E D U S T
            R     A     A       E
      N E R V E     S     N       C
            A     Y     G       O
            T     D           N
            H     O W N         D
                  E           W
            B R U S H         I
                  I     B L I N D
      F E E T W E T         D
```

B. 1. a
    2. b
    3. c
    4. a

    5. c
    6. b
    7. a
    8. b

C. 1. get my second wind
    2. getting your feet wet
    3. get the hang of
    4. hold your own

    5. get up enough nerve
    6. bite the dust
    7. to have a brush with death
    8. easy does it

D. 1. J
    2. C
    3. B
    4. D
    5. H

    6. I
    7. E
    8. A
    9. F
    10. G

LESSON EIGHT - *Paul's eyes are "bigger than his stomach"*

Practice the Vocabulary

A. 1. tooth
   2. eye
   3. weakness
   4. stomach

   5. pull
   6. world
   7. thin
   8. heads

B. 1. tooth
   2. eyes
   3. air
   4. weakness

   5. strings
   6. tails
   7. stick
   8. eye

C. 1. H
   2. C
   3. G
   4. F

   5. D
   6. E
   7. A
   8. B

D. 1. weakness
   2. pull
   3. world
   4. pad
   5. stomach
   6. heads
   7. tooth
   8. stick
   9. catch
   10. thin

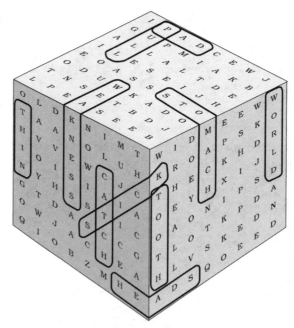

LESSON NINE - *"I'm not going to take this lying down"*

Practice the Vocabulary

A. **CROSSWORD**

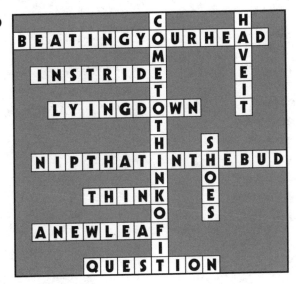

B. 1. b
    2. a
    3. c
    4. b

5. a
6. c
7. c
8. a

C. 1. take this lying down
    2. got another think coming
    3. let him have it
    4. in the bud

5. come to think of it
6. out of the question
7. beating my head
8. in your shoes

D. 1. H
    2. A
    3. D
    4. C

5. G
6. F
7. E
8. B

LESSON TEN - *Sally is "showing her true colors"*

Practice the Vocabulary

A. 1. correct
   2. correct
   3. incorrect
   4. incorrect

   5. correct
   6. incorrect
   7. correct
   8. incorrect

B. 1. gives
   2. short
   3. level
   4. up

   5. colors
   6. off
   7. right
   8. square

C. 1. a
   2. b
   3. a
   4. c

   5. c
   6. c
   7. b
   8. a

D. 1. a
   2. b
   3. a
   4. b

   5. a
   6. b
   7. a
   8. a

REVIEW EXAM FOR LESSONS 6-10

Practice the Vocabulary

A. 1. town
   2. hang
   3. crack
   4. wind
   5. strings

6. stick
7. shoes
8. head
9. one
10. colors

B. **CROSSWORD**

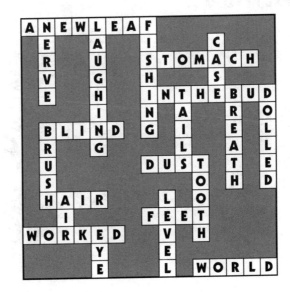

C. 1. False
   2. True
   3. False
   4. False
   5. True

6. False
7. False
8. True
9. False
10. True

D. 1. C
   2. E
   3. I
   4. A
   5. D

6. J
7. B
8. H
9. F
10. G

LESSON ELEVEN - *Jeff finds an interesting "knick-knack"*

Practice the Vocabulary

A. 1. c
   2. b
   3. a
   4. c

   5. c
   6. c
   7. a

B. **FILL-IN BLOCKS**

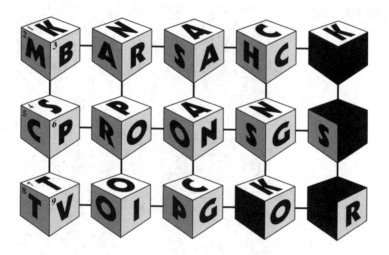

C. 1. span
   2. patter
   3. knacks
   4. mash

   5. crosses
   6. top
   7. tock
   8. vigor

LESSON TWELVE - *Tom is "going toe-to-toe with everyone"*

Practice the Vocabulary

A. 1. correct
   2. incorrect
   3. correct
   4. correct
   5. incorrect
   6. correct
   7. incorrect
   8. incorrect

B. 1. more and more
   2. through-and-through
   3. up-and-up
   4. so-and-so
   5. over-and-over
   6. R-and-R
   7. tête-à-tête
   8. to go toe-to-toe

C. 1. eye-to-eye
   2. over-and-over
   3. more and more
   4. tête-à-tête
   5. R-and-R
   6. out-and-out
   7. through-and-through
   8. up-and-up
   9. so-and-so
  10. toe-to-toe

D. 1. a
   b. b
   3. c
   4. b
   5. a
   6. a
   7. b
   8. a

LESSON THIRTEEN - *"When it rains, it pours"*

Practice the Vocabulary

A. 1. sight
   2. rains
   3. Rome; Romans
   4. bygones

   5. Actions
   6. foot
   7. taste
   8. mile

B. 1. words
   2. mile
   3. Romans
   4. shoe

   5. bygones
   6. mind
   7. pours
   8. taste

C. 1. F
   2. A
   3. E
   4. C

   5. H
   6. G
   7. B
   8. D

LESSON FOURTEEN - *"Freeze!"*

Practice the Vocabulary

A. **CROSSWORD**

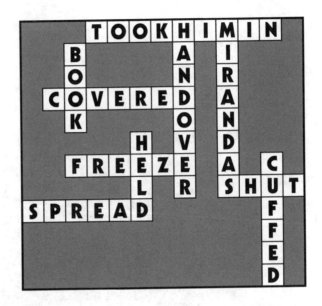

B. 1. c
   2. c
   3. a
   4. a
   5. b
   6. c
   7. a
   8. c

C. 1. Freeze
   2. booked
   3. up
   4. spread
   5. cuffed
   6. Hand
   7. up
   8. covered
   9. Mirandas
   10. in

REVIEW EXAM FOR LESSONS 11-14

Practice the Vocabulary

A. 1. tip-top
   2. up-and-up
   3. bygones be bygones
   4. taste
   5. pours
   6. up
   7. Book
   8. R-and-R

B. **CROSSWORD**

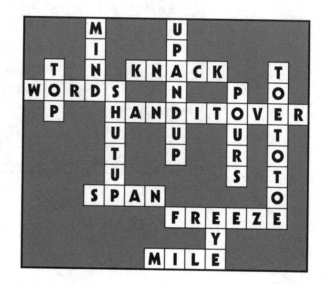

C. 1. False
   2. False
   3. True
   4. True
   5. True
   6. False
   7. False
   8. False
   9. True
   10. True

D. 1. J
   2. B
   3. D
   4. H
   5. I
   6. E
   7. C
   8. F
   9. A
   10. G

APPENDIX
-Dictation- 📼

I'm sure they'll give you a fair shake

[Using reductions, as heard on the audiotape]

T'day I **talked** Debbie inta auditioning fer the school musical. She agreed although she knows she can' even **carry a tune** when she gets nervous. At first, Debbie **broke oudd'n a cold sweat** but then she fin'ly **godda hol'duv 'erself**. Ev'rthing was fine until she saw Nancy walk in. Nancy's the bes' singer in the school. Debbie fin'lly decided ta leave 'cause she knew she wouldn' have a **prayer** if Nancy auditioned.

[As you would see it written]

Today I **talked** Debbie into auditioning for the school musical. She agreed although she knows she can't even **carry a tune** when she gets nervous. At first, Debbie **broke out in a cold sweat** but then she finally **got a hold of herself**. Everything was fine until she saw Nancy walk in. Nancy's the best singer in the school. Debbie finally decided to leave 'cause she knew she wouldn't have a **prayer** if Nancy auditioned.

Lesson 2

It's as plain as the nose on your face

[Using reductions, as heard on the audiotape]

Steve 'n I saw Joe **walking arm 'n arm** with a young woman t'day. I told Steve thad I thought they were **going tagether**. That's when he said I w'z **pulling 'is leg** b'cause she's it least twen'y years younger than Joe. Talk about **robbing the cradle**! I wonder if they'll akshuly **tie the knot**?

[As you would see it written]

Steve and I saw Joe **walking arm in arm** with a young woman today. I told Steve that I thought they were **going together**. That's when he said I was **pulling his leg** because she's at least twenty years younger than Joe. Talk about **robbing the cradle**! I wonder if they'll actually **tie the knot**?

Lesson 3

I think John's getting cold feet

[Using reductions, as heard on the audiotape]

Steve wrecked 'is father's car an' doesn' know how da **break the news** to 'im. His father'll pro'bly **fly off the handle** 'cause 'e had ta **fork over** a lodda money for it. At first, Steve got **cold feet**, but 'e fin'lly decided ta **face the music**.

[As you would see it written]

Steve wrecked his father's car and doesn't know how to **break the news** to him. His father will probably **fly off the handle** 'cause he had to **fork over** a lot of money for it. At first, Steve got **cold feet**, but he finally decided to **face the music**.

Bite your tongue!

[Using reductions, as heard on the audiotape]

Janet's at the **enduv 'er rope** b'cause 'er triplets do nothing b't **scream at the top 'a their lungs** all night. She doesn' **sleep a wink** although 'er husban' manages **ta sleep like a log**. She just hopes she c'n **hang in there** until they're grown up!

[As you would see it written]

Janet's at the **end of her rope** because her triplets do nothing but **scream at the top of their lungs** all night. She doesn't **sleep a wink** although her husband manages **to sleep like a log**. She just hopes she can **hang in there** until they're grown up!

Lesson 5

My house guest is eating me out of house and home

[Using reductions, as heard on the audiotape]

Linda's staying with Tessa fer a week. The problem is that she's **eading Tessa oud of house 'n home**. Tessa's tried talking to 'er but **id all goes in one ear 'n out the other**. What really **gets** Tessa is that Linda keeps walking aroun' the house **'n the raw**. I think Tessa's fin'lly gonna **lay down the law** t'night.

[As you would see it written]

Linda's staying with Tessa for a week. The problem is that she's **eating Tessa out of house and home**. Tessa's tried talking to her but **it all goes in one ear and out the other**. What really **gets** Tessa is that Linda keeps walking around the house **in the raw**. I think Tessa's finally going to **lay down the law** tonight.

Lesson 6

Barbara's having a bad hair day

[Using reductions, as heard on the audiotape]

Barb'ra's having a **bad hair day**. Even **gedding all dolled up** isn't gonna help her. Every time I see 'er, she **gets on my case** 'n **makes cracks** about my clothes. She sher does ged **on my nerves**.

[As you would see it written]

Barbara's having a **bad hair day**. Even **getting all dolled up** isn't gonna help her. Every time I see her, she **gets on my case** and **makes cracks** about my clothes. She sure does get **on my nerves**.

Lesson 7

Jodi's getting the hang of skiing

[Using reductions, as heard on the audiotape]

Jodi's scared she's gonna **bite the dust** when she goes skiing t'morrow. She's never gone b'fore but she's anxious ta **ged 'er feet wet**. I told 'er she'd **get the hang** of id'n five minutes, bud **easy does it** going down the hills. I had a **brush with death** the firs' time I went skiing.

[As you would see it written]

Jodi's scared she's going to **bite the dust** when she goes skiing tomorrow. She's never gone before but she's anxious to **get her feet wet**. I told her she'd **get the hang** of it in five minutes, but **easy does it** going down the hills. I had a **brush with death** the first time I went skiing.

Lesson 8

Paul's eyes are bigger than his stomach

[Using reductions, as heard on the audiotape]

Paul had ta **pull s'm strings** ta get reservations at 'is fav'rite French rest'rant. He 'as a **weakness** fer French food. He says the food is **oud 'a this world**, especially the desserts. Paul's always **had a sweet tooth**. Usually he orders too much food b'cause **'is eyes 'r bigger th'n 'is stomach**.

[As you would see it written]

Paul had to **pull some strings** to get reservations at his favorite French restaurant. He has a **weakness** for French food. He says the food is **out of this world**, especially the desserts. Paul's always **had a sweet tooth**. Usually he orders too much food because **his eyes are bigger th'n his stomach**.

Lesson 9

I'm not going to take this lying down

[Using reductions, as heard on the audiotape]

Dave's brother borrowed 'is car again withoud asking. Dave usually **takes id in stride**, but this time 'e's not gonna **take it lying down**. He's fin'lly gonna **led 'im have it**. He really shud'a **nipped id in the bud** long ago but talking ta Dave's brother is like **beading yer head against a wall**.

[As you would see it written]

Dave's brother borrowed his car again without asking. Dave usually **takes it in stride**, but this time he's not going to **take it lying down**. He's finally going to **let him have it**. He really should've **nipped it in the bud** long ago but talking to Dave's brother is like **beating your head against a wall**.

Lesson 10

Sally is showing her true colors

[Using reductions, as heard on the audiotape]

T'day, Sally **showed 'er true colors** 'n **wen' off on** 'er teacher, Mr. Peders. I've never seen anyone get so **worked up** b'fore. **Ta make a long story short**, Mr. Peders failed 'er b'cuz 'e cod 'er cheading. It's **no laughing madder**. Now she'll have ta take the whole course over again. I can't b'lieve she's gonna have **ta start fr'm square one**.

[As you would see it written]

Today, Sally **showed her true colors** and **went off on** her teacher, Mr. Peters. I've never seen anyone get so **worked up** before. **To make a long story short**, Mr. Peters failed her because he caught her cheating. It's **no laughing matter**. Now she'll have to take the whole course over again. I can't believe she's going to have **to start from square one**.

Lesson 11

Jeff finds an interesting knick-knack

[Using reductions, as heard on the audiotape]

Jeff found 'n int'resting **knick-knack** in a box of **bric-a-brac** Anne's mother's been saving. He w'z saprised ta fin' such a **mish-mash** of junk 'n 'er house b'cuz Anne's mother keeps 'er house **spic-'n- span**.

[As you would see it written]

Jeff found an interesting **knick-knack** in a box of **bric-a-brac** Anne's mother's been saving. He was surprised to find such a **mish-mash** of junk in her house because Anne's mother keeps her house **spic-'n- span**.

Lesson 12

Tom is going toe-to-toe with everyone

[Using reductions, as heard on the audiotape]

More n' more, people 'r having trouble seeing **eye da eye** with Tom. I always thod 'e w'z a great guy **through-'n-through** but lately he's been a real **so-'n-so**. People 'r even starding ta wonder if 'e's on the **up-'n-up**.

[As you would see it written]

More and more, people are having trouble seeing **eye-to-eye** with Tom. I always thought he was a great guy **through-and-through** but lately he's been a real **so-and-so**. People are even starting to wonder if he's on the **up-and-up**.

Lesson 13

When it rains, it pours

[Using reductions, as heard on the audiotape]

I decided **ta let bygones be bygones** 'n be frien's again with Patricia. The problem was that Patricia moved ta Paris, and stopped communicading with me. **Oudda side, oudda mind**. Patricia used ta tell me constantly how much she valued 'R +frien'ship but she never really showed me. I told 'er thad **actions speak louder th'n words**.

[As you would see it written]

I decided **to let bygones be bygones** and be friends again with Patricia. The problem was that Patricia moved to Paris, and stopped communicating with me. **Out of sight, out of mind**. Patricia used to tell me constantly how much she valued our friendship but she never really showed me. I told her that **actions speak louder than words**.

Lesson 14

Freeze!

[Using reductions, as heard on the audiotape]

Yesterday, I wuz **held up**! First I heard someone yell "**Freeze!**" so I stopt. Then a man's voice fr'm b'hin' me said "**Shud up 'n hand over yer wallet**." Jus' then, the police arrived. They **cuft** 'im 'n **took 'im in**. Whad 'n adventure!

[As you would see it written]

Yesterday, I was **held up**! First I heard someone yell "**Freeze!**" so I stopped. Then a man's voice from behind me said "**Shut up** and **hand over your wallet**." Just then, the police arrived. They **cuffed** him and **took him in**. What an adventure!

Glossary

"A friend in need is a friend indeed"
exp. "A friend who is helpful during times of difficulty is a true friend."

usage example: Your best friend could really use your help. Remember, **a friend in need is a friend indeed**.

translation: Your best friend could really use your help. Remember, a friend who is helpful during times of difficulty is a true friend.

"A little knowledge is a dangerous thing" *exp.* "Having only a little information regarding a certain subject could lead to trouble."

usage example: Paul is going to try and fix his own car? He only read one chapter of his auto mechanics book! He's about to prove that **a little knowledge is a dangerous thing.**

translation: Paul is going to try and fix his own car? He only read one chapter of his auto mechanics book! He's about to prove that having a little information about something could lead to trouble.

"A penny saved is a penny earned" *exp.* "It's important to be frugal."

usage example: If I buy shoes at this store, it will cost more than if I bought them at the other store. I know I'll only

be saving a few cents, but **a penny saved is a penny earned**.

translation: If I buy shoes at this store, it will cost more than if I bought them at the other store. I know I'll only be saving a few cents, but it's important to be frugal.

"A watched pot never boils" *exp.* "If you wait for something to happen, it never will."

usage example: I know you're waiting for Mark's telephone call, but you can't just sit next to the telephone all day. You know what they say, "**A watched pot never boils**." Why don't you go do something to keep yourself busy?

translation: I know you're waiting for Mark's telephone call, but you can't just sit next to the telephone all day. You know what they say, "If you wait for something to happen, it never will." Why don't you go do something to keep yourself busy?

"Absence makes the heart grow fonder"
exp. "People, places, and things become more valued the longer they are absent."

usage example: When your boyfriend comes back from his vacation, he'll be even more in love with you. Remember, **absence makes the heart grow fonder**.

translation: When your boyfriend comes back from his vacation, he'll be even more in love with you. Remember, people, places, and things become more valued the longer they are absent.

"Actions speak louder than words" *exp.* "Prove what you say by your actions."

usage example: You always tell me what a good friend I am but every time I need your help, you're always too busy. If I'm really a good friend of yours, show me. **Actions speak louder than words**.

translation: You always tell me what a good friend I am but every time I need your help, you're always too busy. If I'm really a good friend of yours, show me. Prove what you say by your actions.

again and again *exp.* repeatedly.

usage example: I've told you **again and again** to stop bothering me!

translation: I've told you repeatedly to stop bothering me!

"All's fair in love and war" *exp.* "When two people are fighting to win the love of someone else, there are no rules of fair play."

usage example: Mark wants Laura to fall in love with him instead of Tim. So, he lied and told Laura that Tim used to be in prison! I guess **all's fair in love and war**.

translation: Mark wants Laura to fall in love with him instead of Tim. So, he lied and told Laura that Tim used to be in prison! I guess when two people are fighting to win the love of someone else, there are no rules of fair play.

"All's well that ends well" *exp.* "As long as there is a happy outcome to a situation, the struggle to achieve it was worthwhile."

usage example: Mandy lost her house in the fire, but it looks like she'll be able to rebuild an even bigger and better one! **All's well that ends well**.

translation: Mandy lost her house in the fire, but it looks like she'll be able to rebuild an even bigger and better one! As long as there is a happy outcome to a situation, the struggle to achieve it was worthwhile.

another think coming (to have) *exp.* to be destined for an unpleasant surprise.

usage example: If you really believe you're not going to get caught for cheating on the test, you've **got another think coming**.

translation: If you really believe you're not going to get caught for cheating on the test, you're destined for an unpleasant surprise.

NOTE: A common misconception even among native speakers of English is that this expression is *"to have another **thing** coming."* The reason for this is because the letter *"k"* in *"think"* and the *"c"* in *"coming"* share the same sound. Therefore, when pronounced together quickly, *"thing coming"* and *"think coming"* have the same sound.

as plain as the nose on one's face (to be) *exp.* to be obvious.

usage example: I can't believe you have no idea who stole the money from your office. It's **as plain as the nose on your face**!

translation: I can't believe you have no idea who stole the money from your office. It's obvious!

at the end of one's rope (to be) *exp.* to be at the limit of what one can tolerate.

usage example: I've taken my car to the mechanic five times this month and it just stopped working again. I'm **at the end of my rope**!

translation: I've taken my car to the mechanic five times this month and it just stopped working again. I can't tolerate it any more.

at the top of one's lungs (to scream)
exp. to scream as loudly as one can.

usage example: When Cecily saw the attacker, she **screamed at the top of her lungs**. Luckily, that scared him away.

translation: When Cecily saw the attacker, she screamed as loudly as she could. Luckily, that scared him away.

NOTE: Any synonym of the verb "to scream" could be used in this expression such as "to yell," "to shout," "to holler," etc.

B

bad hair day (to have a) *exp.* (very popular) said of someone whose hair looks messy or poorly styled.

usage example: I can't be seen in public today. I'm **having a bad hair day**.

translation: I can't be seen in public today. My hair looks absolutely terrible.

ANTONYM: **to have a good hair day** *exp.*

beat around the bush (to) *exp.* to be indirect and vague.

usage example: Just tell me what you want. Stop **beating around the bush**!

translation: Just tell me what you want. Stop being so indirect and vague!

beat one's head against the wall (to)
exp. to waste one's time trying to achieve something.

usage example: If you're going to try and get our professor to change your grade, you're **beating your head against the wall**.

translation: If you're going to try and get our professor to change your grade, you're wasting your time.

"Beauty is only skin deep" *exp.* "The true measure of beauty is by someone's goodness, not by his or her looks."

usage example: Lana may be beautiful, but she's a terrible person. She sure does prove that **beauty is only skin deep**.

translation: Lana may be beautiful, but she's a terrible person. She sure does prove that the true measure of beauty is by someone's goodness, not his or her looks.

"Beggars can't be choosers" *exp.* "People who are given something for free can't be selective."

usage example: Peter forgot to bring his lunch when we went on our hike, so I offered him some of mine. When I gave him my chicken sandwich, he said he wanted my tuna sandwich instead. I told him that **beggars can't be choosers** and that he could have the chicken sandwich or nothing!

translation: Peter forgot to bring his lunch when we went on our hike, so I offered him some of mine. When I gave him my chicken sandwich, he said he wanted my tuna sandwich instead. I told him that people who are given something for free can't be selective and that he could have the chicken sandwich or nothing!

behind someone's back (to do something) *exp.* to do something secretly and in a malicious manner.

usage example: I just found out that Todd's been talking about me **behind my back**.

translation: I just found out that Todd's been secretly talking about me in a malicious manner.

"Better late than never" *exp.* "It's better to do something late than not to do it at all."

usage example: Although it's late, I wanted to give you this birthday gift. **Better late than never**!

translation: Although it's late, I wanted to give you this birthday gift. It's better to do something late than not to do it at all!

"Better safe than sorry" *exp.* "It's better to do something cautiously or else you may suffer the consequences later."

usage example: I know the piano is far from where we're going to be painting, but we'd better cover it anyway. **Better safe than sorry**.

translation: I know the piano is far from where we're going to be painting, but we'd better cover it anyway. It's better to do something cautiously or else you may suffer the consequences later.

"Birds of a feather flock together" *exp.* "People who are similar attract each other."

usage example: Scott's friends are all strange, but like they say, **birds of a feather flock together**.

translation: Scott's friends are all strange, but like they say, people who are similar attract each other.

NOTE: This expression may simply be shortened to: **birds of a feather** since the rest of the expression is merely inferred.

bite one's tongue (to) *exp.* (figurative) to keep oneself from verbally attacking someone.

usage example: Our new client is so arrogant and insulting, I have to **bite my tongue** around her.

translation: Our new client is so arrogant and insulting, I have to stop myself from verbally attacking her.

ALSO: **"Bite your tongue!"** *exp.* "Don't even suggest the possibility of something so dreadful happening!"

usage example: "Your house guest may never leave." **"Bite your tongue!"**

translation: "Your house guest may never leave." "Don't even suggest the possibility of something so dreadful happening!"

bite the dust (to) *exp.* • **1.** to fall (on the ground, looking as if one is eating dust) • **2.** to fail • **3.** to die.

usage example (1): *[to fall]* As I was riding my bike, I lost my balance and **bit the dust**.

translation: As I was riding my bike, I lost my balance and fell.

usage example (2): *[to fail]* I think I really **bit the dust** on the final exam.

translation: I think I really failed the final examination.

NOTE: *"Exam"* is a popular abbreviation for *"examination."*

usage example (3): *[to die]* I just heard my old piano teacher **bit the dust**.

translation: I just heard my old piano teacher died.

NOTE: When this expression is used to mean "to die," its connotation is disrespectful and indifferent.

blind leading the blind (the) *exp.* said of a situation where an inexperienced or incapable person is being instructed by someone equally inexperienced or incapable.

usage example: Jim is teaching Tom how to play tennis? That's a real case of **the blind leading the blind**.

translation: Jim is teaching Tom how to play tennis? That's a real case of an inexperienced person being taught by someone equally inexperienced.

NOTE: *"Talk about..."* is an extremely popular expression meaning "This is certainly an example of..."

"Blood is thicker than water" *exp.* "Loyalty should be to the family first."

usage example: Leon had a choice of moving to another city with his parents, or staying behind with his friends. Since **blood is thicker than water**, he decided to go with his family.

translation: Leon had a choice of moving to another city with his parents, or staying behind with his friends. Since loyalty should be to the family first, he decided to go with his family.

blow someone away (to) *exp.* to shoot someone.

usage example: One move and I'll **blow you away**!

translation: One move and I'll shoot you!

blow something [all] out of proportion (to) *exp.* to exaggerate.

usage example: Mike's airplane trip was a little bumpy but he's been telling everyone the airplane almost crashed! He sure does **blow everything [all] out of proportion**.

translation: Mike's airplane trip was a little bumpy but he's been telling everyone the airplane almost crashed! He sure does exaggerate.

SYNONYM: **to make something into a bigger deal than it is** *exp.*

usage example: Why are you getting so upset just because I'm two minutes late? You're **making this into a bigger deal than it is**.

translation: Why are you getting so upset just because I'm two minutes late? You're exaggerating this entire situation.

boo-boo *exp.* (baby talk) injury.

usage example: Did you get a **boo-boo** when you fell down?

translation: Did you get injured when you fell down?

NOTE: As just demonstrated, when the sound *"boo"* is repeated, it takes on the meaning of "injury." However, as a single syllable *("Boo!"),* it becomes an interjection used to scare someone:

usage example: Stephanie was hiding behind the door. As soon as I walked by, she jumped out and yelled **"Boo!"**

book someone (to) *exp.* to register someone as a suspect at the police station.

usage example: John was **booked** on suspicion of murder.

translation: John was registered at the police station on suspicion of murder.

break out in a cold sweat (to) *exp.* to begin perspiring suddenly due to great fear or anxiety.

usage example: When I heard about the earthquake near my parents' house, I **broke out in a cold sweat**.

translation: When I heard about the earthquake near my parents' house, I began perspiring suddenly (due to anxiety).

NOTE: The expression *"to break out"* means "to develop (a physical condition)."

usage example: I just **broke out** in a rash.

translation: I just developed a rash.

break the news to someone (to) *exp.* to disclose sensitive and emotional information to someone.

usage example: The veterinarian just called and told me my brother's dog died. I don't know how I'm going **to break the news** to him.

translation: The veterinarian just called and told me my brother's dog died. I don't know how I'm going to disclose such emotional information to him.

bric-a-brac *exp.* a group of inexpensive collectible objects, usually displayed in one's home.

usage example: This is some **bric-a-brac** I've collected over the years.

translation: These are some objects I've collected over the years.

broad daylight (in) *exp.* a common expression used when referring to a crime committed in the middle of the day.

usage example: The bank was robbed in **broad daylight**.

translation: The bank was robbed in the middle of the day.

brush with death (to have a) *exp.* to have a near-death experience.

usage example: I hear you almost got hit by a bus yesterday! You really had a **brush with death**.

translation: I hear you almost got hit by a bus yesterday! You really had a near-death experience.

buy into something (to) *exp.* to accept something.

usage example: He gave you nothing but excuses and you **bought into it**!

translation: He gave you nothing but excuses and you accepted it!

SYNONYM: to fall for something *exp.*

usage example: Why do you keep falling for his excuses?

translation: Why do you keep accepting his excuses?

bye-bye *exp.* (commonly pronounced *"ba-bye"*) good-bye.

usage example: **Bye-bye**!

translation: Good-bye!

NOTE: Young children are commonly told to *"wave bye-bye,"* a phrase applied *only* to children. However, adults do frequently used the phrase *"bye-bye"* with other adults, especially on the telephone.

C

carjack (to) *v.* to steal someone's car by use of a weapon.

usage example: I just got **carjacked**!

translation: I just got my car stolen by someone carrying a weapon!

ALSO: carjacking *n.* the act of stealing a car by use of a weapon.

carry a tune (to) *exp.* said of someone who is able to sing on pitch.

usage example: I'm not really a singer but at least I can **carry a tune**.

translation: I'm not really a singer but at least I can sing on pitch.

catch someone's eye (to) *exp.* to attract someone's attention.

usage example: That painting really **caught my eye**.

translation: That painting really attracted my attention.

cheek-to-cheek *exp.* one person's cheek pressed up against another person's cheek.

usage example: I don't think they're just friends. I saw John and Lisa dancing **cheek-to-cheek** all night!

translation: I don't think they're just friends. I saw John and Lisa dancing with their cheeks pressed up against each other all night!

chit-chat *v. & n.* trivial conversation.

usage example (1): [as a verb] Let's go somewhere and **chit-chat** for a while.

translation: Let's go somewhere and converse for a while.

usage example (2): [as a noun] The party was fun. There was lots of **chit-chat** and good food.

translation: The party was fun. There was lots of conversation and good food.

clip-clop *exp.* This refers to the sound made by a horse as it walks on hard ground.

usage example: Do you hear that **clip-clop** sound? There must be a horse nearby.

translation: Do you hear that sound a horse makes as it walks? There must be a horse nearby.

"Close, but no cigar" *exp.* "Being partially accurate is still inaccurate."

usage example: "Watch me shoot this target. I bet I hit it on my first try." **"Close, but no cigar**. Better luck next time."

translation: "Watch me shoot this target. I bet I hit it on my first try." "Being partially accurate is still inaccurate. Better luck next time."

cold feet (to get) *exp.* to lose courage.

usage example: I was going to ask my boss for a raise but as soon as I saw him, I got **cold feet**.

translation: I was going to ask my boss for a raise but as soon as I saw him, I lost courage.

come clean (to) *exp.* to be honest (and confess the truth).

usage example: **Come clean** with me. Did you borrow my car while I was out of town?

translation: Be honest with me. Did you borrow my car while I was out of town?

come to a head (to) *exp.* said of a situation which reaches a critical point; to come to a climax.

usage example: They've been angry with each other for a long time and last night everything **came to a head**. They yelled at each other for an entire hour!

translation: They've been angry with each other for a long time and last night the situation reached a critical point. They yelled at each other for an entire hour!

"Come to think of it..." *exp.* "In thinking about it more..."

usage example: I wonder if it was John who stole your wallet. **Come to think of it**, I did see him with a wallet that looked just like yours!

translation: I wonder if it was John who stole your wallet. In thinking about it more, I did see him with a wallet that looked just like yours!

cop *n.* police officer.

usage example: You're driving too fast and there's a **cop** behind you!

translation: You're driving too fast and there's a police officer behind you!

NOTE (1): This is an abbreviation of the slang term *"copper,"* used only in old gangster movies and in jest, due to the copper badges worn by police officers.

NOTE (2): This is a popular slang term even among police officers.

cover someone (to) *exp.* 1. to aim a gun at someone • 2. to protect someone by using a gun.

usage example: Surrender. **We've got you covered**!

translation: Surrender. We're aiming our guns at you.

NOTE: The difference between definitions 1. and 2. depends on the context.

"Crime doesn't pay" *exp.* "Whatever the outcome, it's not worth the consequences of committing a crime."

usage example: Sheila stole a thousand dollars from work and now she's going to jail. It's the third time she's done that to an employer. When will she learn that **crime doesn't pay**?

translation: Sheila stole a thousand dollars from work and now she's going to jail. It's the third time she's done that to an employer. When will she learn that it's not worth the consequences of committing a crime?

criss-cross • 1. (noun) a pattern or design made of crossing lines • 2. (verb) to cross.

usage example: Last night, my mother wore a blue dress with a **criss-cross** pattern on the front.

translation: Last night, my mother wore a blue dress with a design made of crossing lines on the front.

cuff someone (to) *exp.* to put handcuffs on someone.

usage example: **Cuff 'im**!

translation: Put handcuffs on him!

NOTE: *"'Im"* is a common reduction for "him."

cuff someone (to) *exp.* to put handcuffs on someone.

usage example: **Cuff 'im**.

translation: Put handcuffs on him.

NOTE: *"'Im"* is a common reduction for "him."

"Curiosity killed the cat" *exp.* "People who are too inquisitive and meddlesome can get themselves into trouble."

usage example: "I think that there are some criminals who just moved into the apartment next door to mine. I'm going to go investigate."
"I wouldn't do that if I were you. They could be dangerous! After all, **curiosity killed the cat**!"

translation: "I think that there are some criminals who just moved into the apartment next door to mine. I'm going to go investigate."
"I wouldn't do that if I were you. They could be dangerous! After all, people who are too inquisitive and meddlesome can get themselves into trouble!"

D

D.U.I. *exp.* a citation for Driving Under the Influence (of alcohol).

usage example: I'm issuing you a **D.U.I.**

translation: I'm issuing you a citation for **d**riving **u**nder the **i**nfluence of alcohol.

VARIATION: D.W.I. *exp.* a citation for **d**riving **w**hile **i**ntoxicated.

ding-dong *n.* This refers to the sound made by a ringing bell.

usage example: Did you hear that **ding-dong** sound? I think someone is at your front door.

translation: Did you hear that bell sound? I think someone is at your front door.

dolled up (to get all) *exp.* to get all dressed up.

usage example: I told her that we were only going to a barbecue but she still wanted **to get all dolled up**.

translation: I told her that we were only going to a barbecue but she still wanted to get all dressed up.

NOTE: This expression is used to describe women only. For both men and women, a common expression is: **to get all decked out**.

SYNONYM: to be dressed to kill *exp.* to be dressed beautifully (may be applied to both men and women).

usage example: Laura was **dressed to kill** tonight!

translation: Laura was all dressed up tonight!

"Don't count your chickens before they hatch" *exp.* "Don't assume success until it actually happens."

usage example: "My job interview went so well today that I'm going to quit my current job!"
"Now, wait! **Don't count your chickens before they hatch**!"

translation: "My job interview went so well today that I'm going to quit my current job!"
"Now, wait! Don't assume success until it actually happens!"

VARIATION (1): Don't count your chickens before they've hatched *exp.*

VARIATION (2): Don't go counting your chickens before they hatch/ they're hatched *exp.*

"Don't hold your breath" *exp.* "Don't anticipate that happening."

usage example: I know she said she'd remember to take you to the airport, but **don't hold your breath**. She forgets everything!

translation: I know she said she'd remember to take you to the airport, but don't anticipate that happening. She forgets everything!

"Don't look a gift horse in the mouth"
exp. "Don't criticize gifts that you receive."

usage example: "I wanted a red bicycle for my birthday. This one is green!" **"Don't look a gift horse in the mouth**. You could have received nothing!"

translation: "I wanted a red bicycle for my birthday. This one is green!" "Don't criticize the gifts that you receive. You could have received nothing!"

"Don't put all your eggs in one basket"
exp. "Don't gamble your possibility of success on one goal since failure could mean losing everything."

usage example: "If I get this job, I can pay off my debts. Then I'll buy a car, new clothes and move to a new apartment." **"Don't put all your eggs in one basket**. What if you don't get the job?"

translation: "If I get this job, I can pay off my debts. Then I'll buy a car, new clothes and move to a new apartment." "Don't gamble your possibility of success on one goal since failure could mean losing everything. You need to apply for several jobs!"

"Don't put the cart before the horse"
exp. "Don't do things out of order."

usage example: You're going to buy a wedding ring before you ask Jan to marry you? **Don't put the cart before the horse**!

translation: You're going to buy a wedding ring before you ask Jan to marry you? Don't do things out of order!

door-to-door (to go) *exp.* to solicit each house in a neighborhood (in hopes of selling a product).

usage example: The salesperson went **door-to-door** trying to sell brushes.

translation: The salesperson went to each house in the neighborhood trying to sell brushes.

NOTE: **door-to-door salesperson** *n.* a merchant who goes to each house in a neighborhood trying to selling products.

E

ear-to-ear *exp.* from one ear to the other.

usage example: When I walked in, my mother was smiling from **ear-to-ear**.

translation: When I walked in, my mother had an enormous smile on her face.

"Early to bed, early to rise makes a man healthy, wealthy, and wise" *exp.* "People who go to bed early are healthier, wealthier, and wiser than people who go to bed late."

usage example: "You're going to bed already? It's only eight o'clock!" "You know what they say. **Early to bed, early to rise makes a man healthy, wealthy, and wise**."

translation: "You're going to bed already? It's only eight o'clock!" "You know what they say. People who go to bed early are healthier, wealthier, and wiser than people who go to bed late."

"Easy come, easy go" *exp.* "Anything that can be easily acquired, can be easily taken away."

usage example: I won a thousand dollars today playing roulette. Then I lost it all on a horse race. Oh, well. **Easy come, easy go.**

translation: I won a thousand dollars today playing roulette. Then I lost it all on a horse race. Oh, well. Anything that can be easily acquired, can be easily taken away.

"Easy does it!" *exp.* • **1.** "Be careful and go slowly!" • **2.** "Calm down!"

usage example: ["Be careful and go slowly!"]
Let's lift this couch on the count of three. But **easy does it**! I know you have a weak back.

translation: Let's lift this couch on the count of three. But be careful! I know you have a weak back.

usage example (2): ["Calm down!"]
Easy does it! I don't like being yelled at like this.

translation: Calm down! I don't like being yelled at like this.

eat someone out of house and home (to) *exp.* to eat all the food in someone's house to the point where the owners can barely afford to buy more food and other essentials.

usage example: My cousin has been staying with us for two months and it's been terrible. He has an enormous appetite. If he stays much longer, he'll **eat us out of house and home**!

translation: My cousin has been staying with us for two months and it's been terrible. He has an enormous appetite. If he stays much longer, we won't be able to afford to live!

"Every [gray] cloud has a silver lining" *exp.* "Bad events are always followed by good events."

usage example: Remember how upset you were last week because you didn't get the job you wanted? Now today, you were offered a job that pays twice as much! **Every [gray] cloud has a silver lining**.

translation: Remember how upset you were last week because you didn't get the job you wanted? Now today, you were offered a job that pays twice as much! Bad events are always followed by good events.

VARIATION: **Behind every [gray] cloud is a silver lining** *exp.*

"Every dog has its/his day" *exp.* "Every person will have his/her moment of glory."

usage example: I just won a thousand dollars! I guess it's true when they say that **every dog has its/his day**!

translation: I just won a thousand dollars! I guess it's true when they say that every person will have his/her moment of glory!

eye-to-eye (to see) *exp.* to be in agreement.

usage example: We don't **see eye-to-eye** on how to raise children.

translation: We don't agree on how to raise children.

eyes bigger than one's stomach (to have) *exp.* to anticipate being able to eat more food than one really can.

usage example: Look at all that food you ordered! I think **your eyes are bigger than your stomach**.

translation: Look at all that food you ordered! I think you anticipated being able to eat more food than you can.

F

face the music (to) *exp.* to confront an uncomfortable situation.

usage example: Our house guest has stayed with us an extra two weeks and he's making us crazy. I've been avoiding asking him to leave but I think it's finally time **to face the music**.

translation: Our house guest has stayed with us an extra two weeks and he's making us crazy. I've been avoiding asking him to leave but I think it's finally time to confront the situation.

face-to-face *exp.* in person.

usage example: I've been looking forward to meeting you **face-to-face**.

translation: I've been looking forward to meeting you in person.

fair shake (to give someone a) *exp.* to give someone the same fair treatment as you would give to others.

usage example : Do you think the jury will give the defendant a **fair shake**?

translation: Do you think the jury will give the defendant a fair trial?

false move *exp.* an incorrect maneuver.

usage example: One **false move** and I'll kill you.

translation: One incorrect maneuver and I'll kill you.

"Familiarity breeds contempt" *exp.*
"Getting to know someone very well

could be dangerous since you may notice unacceptable qualities."

usage example: We were such good friends until we started living together. I guess it's true when they say that **familiarity breeds contempt**.

translation: We were such good friends until we started living together. I guess it's true when they say that getting to know someone very well could be dangerous since you may notice unacceptable qualities.

feet wet (to get one's) *exp.* to try a new experience for the first time.

usage example: I've never played golf before. I'm just **getting my feet wet**.

translation: I've never played golf before. I'm just experiencing it for the first time.

"Finders-keepers, losers-weepers" *exp.* (used primarily among children) "If you find something, you're allowed to keep it even though the person who lost it may cry."

usage example: "Hey, you have my pen! I dropped it here by accident!" "It's mine now. **Finders-keepers, losers-weepers!**"

translation: "Hey, you have my pen! I dropped it here by accident!" "It's mine now. If you find something, you're allowed to keep it."

fish for a compliment from someone (to) *exp.* to try and get a compliment from someone.

usage example: Today Lauren showed me one of the paintings she made. You should have heard her talk for an hour about what a great job she did. She was definitely **fishing for a compliment**.

translation: Today Lauren showed me one of the paintings she made. You should have heard her talk for an hour about what a great job she did. She was definitely trying to get me to compliment her.

fit as a fiddle (to be) *exp.* to be extremely healthy (used mainly by natives of the southern part of the U.S.).

usage example: I was sick yesterday but today I'm **fit as a fiddle**.

translation: I was sick yesterday but today I'm in great health.

flash in the pan (to be a) *exp.* to be quick and temporary.

usage example: His success was only a **flash in the pan**.

translation: His success was only quick and temporary.

flip-flop (to) *exp.* to reverse the order of something.

usage example: The answer to this mathematical problem isn't 32. It's 23. You **flip-flopped** the numbers.

translation: The answer to this mathematical problem isn't 32. It's 23. You reversed the numbers.

ALSO: **flip-flop (to do a)** *exp.* to change dramatically.

usage example: My mom did a real **flip flop** yesterday. She said I couldn't go to the party under any circumstances. Today she said that I could go!

fly off the handle (to) *exp.* to lose one's temper.

usage example: My father **flew off the handle** when the neighbor's dog started barking in the middle of the night.

translation: My father lost his temper when the neighbor's dog started barking in the middle of the night.

fork over (to) *exp.* to pay for something.

usage example: How much money did you have **to fork over** for that new car?

translation: How much money did you have to pay for that new car?

ALSO: **to fork over** *exp.* to give.

usage example: That's mine! **Fork it over!**

translation: That's mine! Give it to me!

"Freeze!" *interj.* "Don't move!"

NOTE: This expression may also be used by police officers.

"Freeze!" *interj.* "Don't move!"

NOTE: This expression may also be used by criminals.

freeze (to) *interj.* to stop and hold completely still.

usage example: **Freeze** or I'll shoot!

translation: Stop and hold completely still or I'll shoot!

frisk someone (to) *exp.* to search someone's clothing for hidden or illegal possessions.

usage example: The police officer **frisked** the man for drugs.

translation: The police officer searched the man for hidden drugs.

frou-frou *exp.* elaborate.

usage example: Did you see the way Susie decorated her house? It's too **frou-frou** for me.

translation: Did you see the way Susie decorated her house? It's too elaborate for me.

G

ga-ga over someone or something (to go) *exp.* to become infatuated by someone or something.

usage example: The first time I saw Rachelle, I went **ga-ga** over her. Isn't she beautiful?

translation: The first time I saw Rachelle, I became infatuated with her. Isn't she beautiful?

NOTE: You may occasionally hear *"ga-ga"* used in conjunction with *"goo-goo." "Goo-goo, ga-ga!"* is commonly used by adults as they talk to babies in an effort to imitate the sound they make.

get [all] worked up about something (to) *exp.* to become very upset about something.

usage example: Just because Nancy spilled the milk, you don't have **to get [all] worked up about it**. I'll have it cleaned up in a minute!

translation: Just because Nancy spilled the milk, you don't have to get so upset about it. I'll have it cleaned up in a minute!

VARIATION: to get [all] worked up over something *exp.*

get a hold of oneself (to) *exp.* to get control of one's emotions.

usage example : **Get a hold of yourself**! I've never seen you so upset before!

translation: Get control of your emotions! I've never seen you so upset before!

SYNONYM (1): to get a grip *exp.*

usage example: **Get a grip**!

translation: Get control of yourself!

SYNONYM (2): to pull oneself together *exp.*

usage example: You've got **to pull yourself together**!

translation: You've got to get control of your emotions!

get on someone's case (to) *exp.* to criticize someone.

usage example: Why do you always have **to get on my case** every time I make a little mistake?

translation: Why do you always have to criticize me every time I make a little mistake?

get on someone's nerves (to) *exp.* to annoy someone.

usage example: That loud music is **getting on my nerves**!

translation: That loud music is annoying me!

get on the stick (to) *exp.* to become more efficient and speedier.

usage example: **Get on the stick**! We have to leave here in five minutes!

translation: Hurry! We have to leave here in five minutes!

get someone (to) *exp.* to annoy someone.

usage example: It really **gets me** when people lie!

translation: It really annoys me when people lie!

VARIATION: to get to someone *exp.* to annoy or to upset.

usage example: He's starting **to get to me**.

translation: He's starting to annoy (or upset) me.

get the hang of something (to) *exp.* to learn how to do something.

usage example: When I first went skiing, I kept falling down. But after a few hours, I started **to get the hang of it**!

translation: When I first went skiing, I kept falling down. But after a few hours, I started to learn how to ski better!

get up enough nerve to do something (to) *exp.* to summon the courage to do something.

usage example: I couldn't **get up enough nerve** to tell him he was fired.

translation: I couldn't summon enough courage to tell him he was fired.

VARIATION: **to get up the nerve to do something** *exp.*

"Gimme your money/wallet/etc." *exp.* "Give me your money/wallet/etc."

NOTE: *"Gimme"* is a common reduction of "give me."

"Give 'im 'iz Mirandas" *exp.* "Give him his Miranda rights."

NOTE (1): *"'Iz"* is a common reduction for "his."

VARIATION (1): **"Read 'im 'iz Mirandas"** *exp.*

VARIATION (2): **"Mirandize 'im"** *exp.*

VARIATION (3): **"Read 'im 'iz rights"**

NOTE (2): *"Miranda rights"* originated from a court case where a suspect (with the last name of Miranda) incriminated himself. Since forcing a suspect to incriminate him/herself is a violation of constitutional rights, the judge in this case declared that any suspect must be read his/her constitutional rights before questioning can be started. These rights are called the *"Miranda rights"* or *"Mirandas."*

The Miranda rights are as follows:

You have the right to remain silent. If you give up the right to remain silent, anything you say can and will be used against you in a court of law. You have the right to speak with an attorney and to have an attorney present during questioning. If you so desire and cannot afford one, an attorney will be appointed for you without charge before questioning.

• *Do you understand each of these rights that I have explained to you?*
• *Do you wish to give up your right to remain silent?*
• *Do you wish to give up your right to speak to an attorney and have him present during questioning?*

"Give 'im 'iz Mirandas" *exp.* "Give him his Miranda rights."

NOTE (1): *"'Iz"* is a common reduction for "his."

VARIATION (1): **"Read 'im 'iz Mirandas"** *exp.*

VARIATION (2): **"Mirandize 'im"** *exp.*

VARIATION (3): **"Read 'im 'iz rights"** *exp.*

"Give someone an inch, he/she will take a mile" *exp.* "If you give someone a little of something, he/she will try to take a lot more."

usage example: I let my sister borrow my dress for the evening. Now she wants to take it with her on vacation for a week! **Give her an inch, she'll take a mile**.

translation: I let my sister borrow my dress for the evening. Now she wants to take it with her on vacation for a week! If you give her a little of something, she'll try to take a lot more.

NOTE: This expression may simply be shortened to: **"Give someone an inch"** since the rest of the expression is merely inferred.

go [off] without a hitch (to) *exp.* said of a project or event that proceeds smoothly.

usage example: Last night was the first time I ever made dinner for my entire family. I have to admit that it went **[off] without a hitch**.

translation: Last night was the first time I ever made dinner for my entire family. I have to admit that there were no problems at all.

SYNONYM: **to go without a snag** *exp.* ["*snag*" = (lit); a break or tear in fabric].

go in one ear and out the other (to) *exp.* to ignore what someone says; not to pay attention to what someone says.

usage example: I've told you three times to take off your shoes before you walk on the new carpet. I feel like everything I say to you **goes in one ear and out the other**.

translation: I've told you three times to take off your shoes before you walk on the new carpet. I feel like you ignore everything I say to you.

go off on someone (to) *exp.* to yell angrily at someone.

usage example: If he says anything about my weight, I'm going **to go off on him**.

translation: If he says anything about my weight, I'm going to yell at him.

go off the deep end (to) *exp.* • **1.** to become upset and irrational • **2.** to become crazy.

usage example: My teacher **went off the deep end** because I was late to class again.

translation: My teacher got really upset because I was late to class again.

SYNONYM: **to flip out** *exp.*

usage example: Sandra **flipped out** when she saw her boyfriend with another woman.

translation: Sandra became extremely upset when she saw her boyfriend with another woman.

go together (to) *exp.* to be dating on a steady basis (said of two people in a relationship).

usage example: Jan and Paul are getting married? I didn't even know they were **going together**!

translation: Jan and Paul are getting married? I didn't even know they were dating each other!

goochy-goo *exp.* These words are used to indicate that someone is being tickled.

usage example: Your baby is so cute! **Goochy-goo!**

translation: Your baby is so cute! Tickle, tickle!

VARIATION (1): **goochy-goochy-goo** *exp.*

VARIATION (2): **coochy-[coochy] coo** *exp.*

goochy-goochy *exp.* tickle, tickle.

usage example: I'm going to tickle you! **Goochy-goochy!**

translation: I'm going to tickle you! Tickle, tickle!

NOTE: This phrase is commonly used by someone who is tickling someone else.

VARIATION (1): goochy-goochy-goo *exp.*

VARIATION (2): coochy-coochy-coo *exp.*

go to town (to) *exp.* to do something to the extreme.

usage example: That saxophonist really **went to town** on his solo!

translation: That saxophonist really played his solo with complete abandon!

SYNONYM (1): to go all out *exp.*

usage example: You really **went all out** for this party!

translation: You really spared no expense for this party!

SYNONYM (2): to let out all the stops *exp.*

usage example: When Joanne gives a party, she **lets out all the stops!**

translation: When Joanne has a party, she goes all the way!

H

ha-ha *exp.* used to indicate laughter (usually sarcastically).

usage example: "What did you think of my joke?"
"**Ha-ha**. Very funny."

ALSO: Ha-ha! *exp.* used to indicate contempt for someone else's misfortune.

usage example: **Ha-ha**! I won and you lost!

SYNONYM: hee-hee *exp.*

hand over something (to) *exp.* to surrender something (to someone).

usage example: **Hand over** your wallet!

translation: Surrender your wallet!

VARIATION: to hand something over *exp.*

usage example: **Hand it over**!

translation: Surrender it (to me)!

hand over something (to) *exp.* to surrender something (to someone).

usage example: **Hand over** your wallet!

translation: Surrender your wallet!

VARIATION: to hand something over *exp.*

usage example: **Hand** your wallet **over**!

translation: Surrender your wallet!

hand-in-hand (to walk) *exp.* to walk while holding hands with someone.

usage example: They must be very good friends. They're **walking hand-in-hand**.

translation: They must be very good friends. They're walking and holding each other's hands.

ALSO: to go hand-in-hand *exp.* to go together.

usage example: Do you think that being rich and being happy **go hand-in-hand**?

translation: Do you think that being rich and being happy go together?

hand-to-hand combat *exp.* fighting with one's hands (as opposed to using weapons).

usage example: The two teams got involved in **hand-to-hand combat**.

translation: The two teams fought each other by use of their hands.

"Hands b'hin' d'jer head/back!" *exp.*
"Hands behind your head back!"

NOTE (1): "B'hin'" is a common
reduction for "behind". In the example
above, the native-born speaker will
either say *"b'hin' d'jer"* or *"b'hind yer"*
at his/her discretion.

NOTE (2): *"D'jer"* is a common
reduction for "your" when preceded by
the letter "D." For example: *I think you
dropped your keys behin'* **d'jer** (or
behind yer) car.

NOTE (3): *"T'cher"* is a common
reduction for "your" when preceded by
the letter "T." For example: *Put* **t'cher**
sweater in the closet.

NOTE (4): *"Yer"* is a common
reduction for "your" when preceded by
any letter. For example: *Where's* **yer**
sister today? • *Is that* **yer** (or **t'cher**)
watch?
It is important to note that *"yer"* and
"y'r" can always be used as a reduction
for "your" or "you're." However, when
preceded by the letter "D" or "T" (as
previously demonstrated), the speaker
has the choice of an additional reduction.

hang in there (to) *exp.* • **1.** to wait
patiently • **2.** to be strong and persevere.

usage example: I'll be over to get you
in about an hour, so just **hang in there**.

translation: I'll be over to get you in
about an hour, so just wait patiently.

"Haste makes waste" *exp.* "If you do
something in a hurry, you'll ruin it (and
you'll probably have to do it over)."

usage example: I know you want to
leave early, but take your time with
these calculations. Remember, **haste
makes waste**.

translation: I know you want to leave
early, but take your time with these

calculations. Remember, if you do the
job in a hurry, you'll make mistakes.

**have a good head on one's shoulders
(to)** *exp.* said of someone who is very
intelligent and rational.

usage example: Tom **has a good
head on his shoulders**. I'm sure he'll
make the right decision about which
house to buy.

translation: Tom is very intelligent and
rational. I'm sure he'll make the right
decision about which house to buy.

have a sweet tooth (to) *exp.* to love
sweets.

usage example: I have a **sweet tooth**.
I could eat candy for every meal!

translation: I love sweets. I could eat
candy for every meal!

have a weakness for something (to) *exp.*
to have a passion for something.

usage example: I **have a weakness** for
chocolate.

translation: I have a passion for
chocolate!

SYNONYM: **to have a thing for
something** *exp.*

usage example: I **have a thing** for the
pastries they serve in this restaurant.

translation: I have a passion for the
pastries they serve in this restaurant.

have the time of one's life (to) *exp.* to
have the best time in one's life.

usage example: I had **the time of my
life** at your party last night!

translation: I had the best time ever at
your party last night!

"He who laughs last, laughs longest" *exp.*
"You did something bad to me, but now

I'm going to do something even worse to you."

usage example: Steve kept laughing about the trick he played on me. But I told him that he'd better stop laughing because **he who laughs last, laughs longest**.

translation: Steve kept laughing about the trick he played on me. But I told him that he'd better stop laughing because I'm going to do something worse to him.
VARIATION: **"He who laughs last, laughs best"** _exp._

head-to-head(to go) _exp._ to fight verbally or physically (like two rams that battle by thrusting their heads against each other).

usage example: Mark and Paul went **head-to-head** for an hour over who should be allowed to go on vacation first.

translation: Mark and Paul fought for an hour over who should be allowed to go on vacation first.

heart-to-heart _exp._ an honest and open conversation.

usage example: We need to have a **heart-to-heart** about sex.

translation: We need to have an honest and open conversation about sex.

"Hip-hip-hooray!" _exp._ a common cheer.

usage example: Let's hear it for our hero! **Hip-hip-hooray**!

"Hit the dirt!" _exp._ "Get down on the ground!"
VARIATION: **"Hit the ground!"** _exp._
NOTE: This expression may also be used by police officers.

"Hit the dirt!" _exp._ "Get down on the ground!"
VARIATION: **"Hit the ground!"** _exp._
NOTE: This expression may also be used by criminals.

hit the nail [right] on the head(to) _exp._ to be absolutely correct.

usage example: "How did he get to be promoted to supervisor? His father must be the president of the company." "I think you **hit the nail [right] on the head**!"

translation: "How did he get to be promoted to supervisor? His father must be the president of the company." "I think you're absolutely correct!
SYNONYM: **to be dead on** _exp._

usage example: You were **dead on** when you said not to trust her. She stole hundreds of dollars from the company!

translation: You were absolutely correct when you said not to trust her. She stole hundreds of dollars from the company!
ANTONYM: **to be way off base** _exp._ to be absolutely incorrect.

usage example: If you think David's going to give you a present, you're **way off base**.

translation: If you think David's going to give you a present, you're absolutely wrong.

hold one's own (to) _exp._ to be very capable at something (without any assistance).

usage example: Doug **holds his own** as an airplane pilot.

translation: Doug is very capable as an airplane pilot.
NOTE (1): The phrase _"when it comes to"_ (meaning "with regard to") commonly follows this expression.

usage example: I can hold my own **when it comes to golf**.

translation: I am capable with regard to golf.

NOTE (2): The phrase *"in the [verb+ing] department"* may also follow this expression.

usage example :   I can hold my own **in the golfing/ singing/cooking/etc. department**.

translation: I am very capable at golfing/singing/ cooking/etc.

hold someone up (to) *exp.* to rob someone.

usage example: I got **held up** today in front of my house!

translation: I got robbed today in front of my house!

ALSO: **to hold someone up at gunpoint** *exp.* to rob someone by using a gun.

hold someone up (to) *exp.* to rob someone.

usage example: I got **held up** in broad daylight!

translation: I got robbed in the middle of the day!

NOTE: The expression *"in broad daylight"* is commonly used when talking about crimes committed in the middle of the day.

ALSO: **to hold someone up at gunpoint** *exp.* to rob someone by using a gun.

hold-up *exp.* robbery.

usage example: This is a **hold-up**. Don't anyone move!

translation: This is a robbery. Don't anyone move!

NOTE (1): This expression was originated since victims are made to

"hold up" their arms during a robbery to show that they are not carrying weapons.

SYNONYM: SEE: **stick up** *exp.*

ALSO: SEE: **to hold someone up** *exp.*

"Honesty is the best policy" *exp.* "You'll always get the best results if you're honest."

usage example: You'd better confess the truth to your mother. **Honesty is the best policy**.

translation: You'd better confess the truth to your mother. You'll always get the best results if you're honest.

I

"I'll blow your head off!" *exp.* "I'll shoot you in the head!"

usage example: Don't move or **I'll blow your head off**!

translation: Don't move or I'll shoot you in the head!

I'll say! *exp.* • **1.** "Absolutely!" • **2.** "You're absolutely right!"

usage example: "Do you think he's handsome?" **"I'll say!"**

translation: "Do you think he's handsome?" "Absolutely!"

NOTE: When pronouncing this expression, it's important to put the emphasis on *"I'll"* giving it a higher pitch than *"say."*

"If at first you don't succeed, try, try again" *exp.* "If you don't succeed in doing something the first time, keep on trying."

usage example: What do you mean you're ready to give up? **If at first you don't succeed, try, try again**.

translation: What do you mean you're ready to give up? If you don't succeed in doing something the first time, keep on trying.

"If worse comes to worst..." _exp._ "In the worst possible case..."

usage example: I'm sure we'll be able to get a ticket on the airplane. Besides, **if worse comes to worst**, we can always take a train.

translation: I'm sure we'll be able to get a ticket on the airplane. Besides, in the worst possible case, we could always take a train.

SYNONYM: **"If push comes to shove"** _exp._

in someone's shoes (to be) _exp._ to be in someone else's situation.

usage example: Your rent is due in two weeks! If I were **in your shoes**, I'd be looking for a job today instead of going to the movies.

translation: Your rent is due in two weeks! If I were in your situation, I'd be looking for a job today instead of going to the movies.

in the raw (to be) _exp._ to be completely naked.

usage example: I guess he didn't know I was in the house. When I walked into the living room, he was just standing there **in the raw**!

translation: I guess he didn't know I was in the house. When I walked into the living room, he was just standing there completely naked!

SYNONYM: **to be in one's birthday suit** _exp._ (humorous) • (lit); to be dressed

the same way as one is at the moment of birth; naked.

"It takes two to tango" _exp._ "It takes two people to do certain activities."

usage example: What do you mean the fight was my fault? **It takes two to tango**!

translation: What do you mean the fight was my fault? It takes two people to have a fight!

J

---

jingle-jangle _exp._ The sound made by metallic objects rubbing against each other.

usage example: Do you have keys in your pocket? I hear a **jingle-jangle** sound as you walk.

translation: Do you have keys in your pocket? I hear a jingling sound as you walk.

junk-food junkie _exp._ a person who loves unhealthful food such as candies, cookies, fried foods, etc.

usage example: I admit that I'm a **junk-food junkie**. I could eat cookies all day!

translation: I admit that I love unhealthful food. I could eat cookies all day!

K

---

keep someone posted (to) _exp._ to keep someone informed.

usage example: I'm not sure when I'll be arriving at the airport, but I should know tomorrow. I'll **keep you posted**.

translation: I'm not sure when I'll be arriving at the airport, but I should know tomorrow. I'll keep you informed.

keep something to oneself (to) *exp.* to keep something secret.

usage example: You have **to keep this to yourself**. I just found out that Maggie won the election but it won't be announced until tomorrow.

translation: You have to keep this secret. I just found out that Maggie won the election but it won't be announced until tomorrow.

"Keep yer hands where I c'n see 'em" *exp.*

NOTE (1): *"Yer"* is a common reduction of "your."

NOTE (2): *"C'n"* is a common reduction of "can."

NOTE (3): *"'Em"* is a common reduction of "them."

NOTE (4): This expression may also be used by police officers and criminals.

knick-knack *exp.* a name given to an insignificant object or trinket; a "thing."

usage example: How long have you been collecting these **knick-knacks**?

translation: How long have you been collecting these things?

VARIATION: **nicknack** *exp.*

L

lay down the law (to) *exp.* to impose strict rules.

usage example: I'm tired of you kids coming to my house and misbehaving! Now I'm **laying down the law**. There will be no jumping, no yelling, and no hitting while you're in my home. Is that clear?

translation: I'm tired of you kids coming to my house and misbehaving! Now I'm imposing strict rules. There will be no jumping, no yelling, and no hitting while you're in my home. Is that clear?

"Lemme see yer hands" *exp.* "Let me see your hands."

NOTE (1): *"Lemme"* is a common reduction for "let me."

NOTE (2): *"Yer"* is a common reduction for "your."

"Let bygones be bygones" *exp.* "Let's forget what happened in the past (and look toward the future)."

usage example: I know you had a big fight with Julie a long time ago. Maybe it's time to **let bygones be bygones** and be friends again.

translation: I know you had a big fight with Julie a long time ago. Maybe it's time to forget about what happened in the past and be friends again.

let someone have it (to) *exp.* to reprimand someone strongly.

usage example: If he insults me again, I'm going **to let him have it**!

translation: If he insults me again, I'm going to reprimand him.

SYNONYM: **to give it to someone** *exp.*

usage example: My mother **gave it** to my brother for using her car without permission.

usage example: If he insults me again, I'm going **to let him have it**!

translation: If he insults me again, I'm going to reprimand him.

SYNONYM: to give it to someone *exp.*

usage example: My mother **gave it** to my brother for using her car without permission.

translation: My mother reprimanded my brother for using her car without permission.

let someone have it (to) *exp.* to kill someone (either figuratively or literally, depending on the context).

usage example: If you don't gimme yer money right now, I'm gonna **let cha have it**!

translation: If you don't give me your money right now, I'm going to kill you!

NOTE: *"Let cha"* and *"let chew"* are a common reductions of "let you."

let someone off the hook (to) *exp.* to release someone of responsibility.

usage example: I know you broke my watch by accident, so I'm going **to let you off the hook**. Just be careful next time.

translation: I know you broke my watch by accident, so I'm not going to hold you responsible. Just be careful next time.

NOTE: This expression may also be shortened to **to let someone off** *exp.*

usage example: I'll **let you off** this one time.

translation: I'll release you of responsibility this one time.

SYNONYM: to let someone slide *exp.*

"Let's take 'im in 'n book 'im" *exp.* "Let's take him into the police station and register him."

NOTE: to book someone *exp.* to register someone as a suspect by putting his/her name into a logbook at the police station.

"Live and let live" *exp.* "Live your own life without telling others how to live theirs."

usage example: Why do you care how my friends live their lives. It's none of your business. **Live and let live**.

translation: Why do you care how my friends live their lives. It's none of your business. Live your own life without telling others how to live theirs.

love at first sight (to be) *exp.* said of a situation where two people fall in love upon first glance.

usage example: With my mom and dad, it was **love at first sight**.

translation: With my mom and dad, they fell in love as soon as they saw each other.

lu-lu (to be a) *exp.* said of something impressive.

usage example: How did you get that black eye? What a **lu-lu**!

translation: How did you get that black eye? How impressive!

M

make cracks about someone or something (to) *exp.* to make derogatory remarks about someone or something.

usage example: If you **make another crack** about my best friend, I'll never speak to you again.

usage example: Welcome to my house. Please **make yourself at home**.

translation: Welcome to my house. Please make yourself feel as comfortable as you would in your own home.

mish-mash *exp.* a collection of unrelated items or elements.

usage example: At the party last night, they served a **mish-mash** of different foods. The appetizers were Ethiopian, the main course was a French delicacy, the vegetables were prepared Spanish style, and the desserts were all Greek.

translation: At the part last night, they served a variety of different foods. The appetizers were Ethiopian, the main course was a French delicacy, the vegetables were prepared Spanish style, and the desserts were all Greek.

"Money is the root of all evil" *exp.* "Money causes all the problems in the world."

usage example: A lot of people will do anything for money even if it hurts others. I think it's true when people say that **money is the root of all evil**.

translation: A lot of people will do anything for money even if it hurts others. I think it's true when people say that money causes all of the problems in the world.

more and more *exp.* increasingly often.

usage example (1): **More and more**, people are moving to California.

translation: Increasingly often, people are moving to California.

usage example (2): There's a lot of crime in our city. It's happening **more and more**.

translation: There's a lot of crime in our city. It's happening increasingly often.

NOTE (1): As seen above, when followed by a comma (or pause), the expression *"more and more"* means "increasingly often." However, if not followed by a comma (or pause), the expression means "an increasing amount." For example:

More and more, *people are moving to California.*

Increasingly often, people are moving to California.

More and more *people are moving to California.*

An increasing number of people are moving to California.

NOTE (2): When followed by a comma (or pause), the expression *"less and less"* means "increasingly seldom." However, if not followed by a comma (or pause), the expression means "a decreasing amount." For example:

Less and less, *people are buying cars.*

Decreasingly often, people are buying cars.

Less and less *people are buying new cars.*

A decreasing number of people are buying new cars.

mouth-to-mouth *exp.* (short for *"mouth-to-mouth resuscitation"*) a resuscitation technique used on someone who has stopped breathing - the technique consists of pressing the rescuer's mouth against the victim's mouth and blowing air into his/her lungs.

usage example: I had to give **mouth-to-mouth** to my little brother when he fell into the swimming pool and stopped breathing.

translation: I had to resuscitate my little brother when he fell into the swimming pool and stopped breathing.

muu-muu *n.* a long cool one-piece dress (originally worn by women in Hawaii - pronounced "moo-moo").

usage example: I bought this **muu-muu** in Hawaii. It'll be perfect to wear when I go to parties this summer.

translation: I bought this cool long one-piece dress in Hawaii. It'll be perfect to wear when I go to parties this summer.

N

"Naughty, naughty!" *exp.* a phrase used primarily by parents when scolding a disobedient child.

usage example: **Naughty, naughty!** I told you not to touch that!

"Necessity is the mother of invention" *exp.* "If you're desperate enough, you'll find a way to accomplish anything."

usage example: I couldn't afford to take my car to the mechanic so, I figured out a way to fix my car for free. **Necessity is the mother of invention**.

translation: I couldn't afford to take my car to the mechanic so, I figured out a way to fix my car for free. If you're desperate enough, you'll find a way to accomplish anything.

neck-and-neck (to be) *exp.* to be even in a race.

usage example: The two runners are **neck-and-neck**. I wonder who will finally be the winner!

translation: The two runners are even. I wonder who will finally be the winner!

nip something in the bud (to) *exp.* to put a stop to something quickly before it has a chance to get worse (as one would stop the growth of a flower by clipping or "nipping" the bud).

usage example: The children were starting to fight over the ball so I **nipped it in the bud** by taking it away.

translation: The children were starting to fight over the ball so I put a stop to it quickly by taking it away.

no laughing matter (to be) *exp.* said of a serious situation.

usage example: This is **no laughing matter**. If you don't pass this test, you're not going to graduate.

translation: This is a serious situation. If you don't pass this test, you're not going to graduate.

"No news is good news" *exp.* "If you haven't received any news, assume it's good news."

usage example: I had my job interview a week ago and I still haven't heard anything. I hope that doesn't mean I didn't get the job. I have to keep remembering that **no news is good news**.

translation: I had my job interview a week ago and I still haven't heard anything. I hope that doesn't mean I didn't get the job. I have to keep remembering that if you haven't received any news, assume it's good news.

"Nothing ventured, nothing gained" *exp.* "If you don't attempt something difficult, you'll never benefit from the potential rewards."

usage example: I know you're nervous to ask the boss for a raise, but remember, **nothing ventured, nothing gained**.

translation: I know you're nervous to ask the boss for a raise, but remember, if you don't attempt it, you'll never get anything.

no-host bar *exp.* a bar at a party where the guests are expected to pay for their drinks.

usage example: If you want something to drink, you'll have to pay for it. It's a **no-host bar**.

translation: If you want something to drink, you'll have to pay for it. The guests have to pay for their own drinks.
NOTE: The term *"no-host"* bar is only common in the western portion of the United States, whereas the expression *"cash-bar"* is used in the east.

no-no *n.* (used by parents when talking to a child) not permitted.

usage example: Eating ice cream in the living room is a **no-no**!

translation: Eating ice cream in the living room is not permitted!
NOTE (1): Adults frequently use this expression among themselves as well. For example:

usage example: Being late is a big **no-no** in this office.
NOTE (2): Other synonyms for *"no"* would be incorrect in this expression, such as *"nope-nope," "nah-nah,"* etc. Additionally, this expression does not work with *"yes."* Therefore, *"yes-yes," "yep-yep," "uh-huh, uh-huh,"* etc. would all be incorrect usage.

nothing but skin and bones (to be) *exp.* to be excessively thin.

usage example: You're **nothing but skin and bones**! Haven't you been eating well?

translation: You're so thin! Haven't you been eating well?

O

on second thought *exp.* upon reconsideration.

usage example: I think I'll buy this suit right now. **On second thought**, I'd better wait until I have more money.

translation: I think I'll buy this suit right now. Upon reconsideration, I'd better wait until I have more money.

on the level (to be) *exp.* to be telling the truth.

usage example: The salesman said he's giving us the best price in town. Do you think he's **on the level**?

translation: The salesman said he's giving us the best price in town. Do you think he's being truthful?

"On your knees!" *exp.* "Get on your knees!"

on-and-on (to go) *exp.* to talk incessantly.

usage example: Lisa **goes on-and-on** about how she wants to be a big movie star some day.

translation: Lisa talks incessantly about how she wants to be a big movie star some day.

one-by-one *exp.* one person or thing at a time.

usage example: I want you to fold your shirts carefully **one-by-one**.

translation: I want you to fold your shirts carefully one at a time.

"One good turn deserves another" *exp.* "A good deed should be rewarded with another good deed."

usage example: I really appreciate you helping me move yesterday. Since **one good turn deserves another**, I'd like to give you these free airplane tickets to Europe.

translation: I really appreciate you helping me move yesterday. Since one good deed should be rewarded with another, I'd like to give you these free airplane tickets to Europe.

"One's bark is worse than one's bite" *exp.* said of someone who is threatening but not dangerous.

usage example: Our new boss yells a lot but don't worry. **His bark is worse than his bite**.

translation: Our new boss yells a lot but don't worry. He's threatening but not dangerous.

"Out of sight, out of mind" *exp.* "That which you don't see, you don't think about."

usage example: I haven't received a letter from her in over four months and she's my best friend! **Out of sight, out of mind**.

translation: I haven't received a letter from her in over four months and she's my best friend! If I'm not in front of her, she doesn't think of me.

out of this world (to be) *exp.* to be extraordinary.

usage example: This dinner is **out of this world**.

translation: This dinner is extraordinary.

out-and-out *exp.* complete, total (may be used to modify a noun or a verb).

usage example: He's an **out-and-out** liar!

translation: He's a complete liar!

over-and-over *exp.* repeatedly.

usage example: I've told you **over-and-over** to take your shoes off before you walk on the new carpet.

translation: I've told you repeatedly to take your shoes off before you walk on the new carpet.

VARIATION: **over-and-over again** *exp.*

P

pad the bill (to) *exp.* to add extra charges to a bill.

usage example: How could this restaurant bill be so expensive? I wonder if the waiter **padded the bill**.

translation: How could this restaurant bill be so expensive? I wonder if the waiter added extra charges to the bill.

pee-pee (to go) *exp.* (originally baby talk but also used in jest by adults) to urinate.

usage example: I have **to go pee-pee** before we leave.

translation: I have to go urinate before we leave.

ping pong *exp.* table tennis (originally a trademark for table tennis equipment).

usage example: Do you know how to play **ping pong**?

translation: Do you know to play table tennis?

NOTE: **Ping Pong** is a trademark and should be capitalized (although oftentimes it is not).

pitter-patter *exp.* noise made by anything that causes alternating tones (such as rain, footsteps, etc.).

usage example: I love the **pitter-patter** of the rain.

translation: I love the sound the rain makes.

pom-pom *n.* a ball of wool, feathers, or strips of colored paper used as decoration and by cheerleaders (also spelled "*pom-pon*").

usage example: The cheerleaders were waving their **pom-poms** as they cheered the soccer team.

translation: The cheerleaders were waving decorative balls of colored paper as they cheered the soccer team.

pooh-pooh (to go) *n.* (baby talk - pronounced "*POO-poo*" with the emphasis on the first "*poo*") to defecate.

usage example: I think Tessa just **went pooh-pooh** in her diapers.

translation: I think Tessa just defecated in her diapers.

ALSO: **to pooh-pooh something** *exp.* (pronounced "*poo-POO*" with the emphasis on the second "*poo*") to reject something.

usage example: The boss **pooh-poohed** my idea of hiring Steve.

translation: The boss rejected my idea of hiring Steve.

pop the question (to) *exp.* to propose marriage.

usage example: I think Steve is finally going **to pop the question** tonight!

translation: I think Steve is finally going to propose tonight!

"Practice makes perfect" *exp.* "You can only perfect your skills by practicing."

usage example: You need to play the piano at least an hour every day. **Practice makes perfect**.

translation: You need to play the piano at least an hour every day. You can only perfect your skills by practicing.

"Practice what you preach" *exp.* "Take the same advice you give others."

usage example: You always tell me how terrible it is for people to lie, but today you lied to me! Why don't you **practice what you preach**!

translation: You always tell me how terrible it is for people to lie, but today you lied to me! Why don't you take the same advice you give others!

prayer (not to have a) *exp.* to have no possibility of success in something.

usage example: You **don't have a prayer** of beating Andy at chess.

translation: You don't have any possibility of beating Andy at chess.

ANTONYM: **to have a [good] shot at something** *exp.* to have a [good] possibility at success in something.

usage example: Don't you think Dan **has a shot** at getting the job?

translation: Don't you think Dan has a chance of getting the job?

pull some strings (to) *exp.* to use one's influence.

usage example: I'll have **to pull some strings** to get a reservation at this restaurant with such short notice.

translation: I'll have to use my influence to get a reservation at this restaurant with such short notice.

pull someone's leg (to) *exp.* to kid someone; to tease.

usage example: You just found five hundred dollars? Are you **pulling my leg**?

translation: You just found five hundred dollars? Are you kidding me?

"Put 'em up!" *exp.* "Put them up!"

NOTE (1): In this expression, *'em* (short for "them") refers to "the hands."

NOTE (2): This expression may also be used by police officers.

VARIATION: **"Stick 'em up!"** *exp.*

SEE: **stick up** *exp.*

R

R-and-R *exp.* (originally military lingo) rest and recreation (or rest and relaxation).

usage example: I've been working hard. I need some **R-and-R**.

translation: I've been working hard. I need some rest and recreation.

NOTE: The expression *"R and R"* is always pronounced *R 'n R*.

riff-raff *exp.* dishonorable people.

usage example: You like these people? They're nothing but **riff-raff**!

translation: You like these people? They're all totally dishonorable.

right-as-rain *exp.* perfectly fine (used only by natives of the southern part of the U.S.).

usage example: Everything's **right-as-rain**!

translation: Everything's going perfectly fine!

rob the cradle (to) *exp.* to date someone much younger than oneself, to be dating a "baby."

usage example: Karen's date is young enough to be her son. She certainly is **robbing the cradle**!

translation: Karen's date is young enough to be her son. She certainly is dating someone much younger!

S

same old-same old *exp.* same as usual.

usage example: "How's everything going?" **"Same old, same old."**

translation: "How's everything going?" "Same as usual."

second wind (to get one's) *exp.* to get a second burst of energy.

usage example: During the race, I started getting tired after about five minutes. Then all of a sudden, I got **my second wind** and won the race!

translation: During the race, I started getting tired after about five minutes. Then all of a sudden, I got a second burst of energy and won the race!

see-saw *n.* A recreational device on which two children, seated at opposite ends of a long plank balanced in the middle, alternately ride up and down as each exerts his/her weight.

usage example: Let's go play on the **see-saw**!

SYNONYM: **teeter-totter** *n.*

"Seeing is believing" *exp.* "I'll believe it when I see it."

usage example: I didn't believe you were an acrobat but **seeing is believing**!

translation: I didn't believe you were an acrobat but now that I've seen you perform, I believe it!

serve someone right (to) *exp.* to suffer the consequences that one deserves.

usage example: The school isn't going to let Jennifer graduate because she was caught cheating on her final exam. It **serves her right**!

translation: The school isn't going to let Jennifer graduate because she was caught cheating on her final exam. She's getting what she deserves!

ship-shape *exp.* very orderly and clean (originally a nautical term).

usage example: Your house is really **ship-shape**. My house is always so messy.

translation: Your house is really orderly and clean. My house is always so messy.

show one's true colors (to) *exp.* to reveal one's true personality.

usage example: We all thought Cathy was a timid person but when she saved a child from a burning building, she **showed her true colors**.

translation: We all thought Cathy was a timid person but when she saved a child from a burning building, she showed her true personality.

shut up (to) *interj.* to stop talking.

usage example: If you don't **shut up**, I'll kill you!

translation: If you don't stop talking, I'll kill you!

NOTE: The expression *"Shut up!"* is considered rather coarse. The polite form would be *"Please be quiet."*

"Shut up!" *interj.* "Stop talking!"

usage example: **Shut up** or I'll shoot!

translation: Stop talking or I'll shoot!

NOTE: This expression may also be used by criminals.

sing-song *exp.* alternating up and down in pitch.

usage example: Italian and Chinese are very **sing-song** languages.

translation: Italian and Chinese are very musical languages.

sleep a wink (not to) *exp.* not to sleep at all.

usage example: I didn't **sleep a wink** last night.

translation: I didn't sleep at all last night.

sleep like a log (to) *exp.* to sleep soundly.

usage example: I **slept like a log** last night.

translation: I slept soundly last night.

so-and-so *exp.* • **1.** a replacement for the name of a person; someone • **2.** a euphemistic replacement for any vulgar or obscene noun pertaining to a person.

usage example: What would you do if **so-and-so** approached you and demanded all your money?

translation: What would you do if someone approached you and demanded all your money?

NOTE: The expression *"so-and-so"* is always pronounced *so-'n-so*.

so-so *exp.* neither very good nor very bad, passable.

usage example: "How did your job interview go?"
"So-so."

translation: "How did your job interview go?"
"It was passable."

spic-and-span *exp.* extremely clean.

usage example: We have to get the house **spic-and-span** before my relatives come to visit.

translation: We have to get the house completely clean before my relatives come to visit.

spitting image of someone (to be the)
exp. to be identical to someone.

usage example: She's the **spitting image** of her mother.

translation: She looks just like her mother.

NOTE: This expression is commonly pronounced *"to be the spit'n image of someone."*

VARIATION: to be the spit and image of someone *exp.*

usage example: He's the **spit and image** of his father.

translation: He looks just like his father.

spread them (to) *exp.* to spread apart one's arms and legs.

usage example: Lie on the ground and **spread 'em!**

translation: Lie on the ground and spread your arms and legs apart!

NOTE: In this expression, *"'em"* refers to "them" meaning "the arms and legs."

start from square one (to) *exp.* to start from the very beginning.

usage example: There are some parts of your story that I don't understand. **Start from square one**.

translation: There are some parts of your story that I don't understand. Start from the beginning.

"Stay down!" *exp.* "Stay on the ground!"

"Step oudda the vehicle" *exp.* "Get out of the car."

NOTE: *"Outta"* (pronounced *"oudda"*) is a common reduction of "out of."

stick-up *exp.* robbery.

usage example: Did you hear about the **stick up** at the bank today?

translation: Did you hear about the robbery at the bank today?

NOTE: This expression was originated since victims are made to *"stick up"* their arms during a robbery to show that they are not carrying weapons.

such-and-such *exp.* not yet determined.

usage example: We'll all meet tomorrow at **such-and-such** a time.

translation: We'll all meet tomorrow at a time to be determined later.

suspect *n.* one who is under suspicion of having committed a crime.

usage example: You are our prime **suspect**.

translation: You are the person that we most suspect of having committed the crime.

T

ta-ta *exp.* (pronounced "ta-TA" with the emphasis on the second "ta") good-bye.

usage example: See you tomorrow. **Ta-ta**!

translation: See you tomorrow. Good-bye!

take someone in (to) *exp.* to take someone to the police station for processing.

usage example: Let's **take 'im in**.

translation: Let's take him to the police station and process him.

take something in stride (to) *exp.* to accept something without getting upset.

usage example: She didn't seem too upset when her house burned down. She certainly **took it in stride**.

translation: She didn't seem too upset when her house burned down. She certainly accepted it without getting upset.

SYNONYM: **to let it slide** *exp.*

usage example: Don't get so angry! Just **let it slide**.

translation: Don't get so angry! Just accept it without getting upset!

take something lying down (to) *exp.* to accept something passively.

usage example: He just insulted you. Are you going **to take that lying down**?

translation: He just insulted you. Are you going to accept that passively?

talk someone into something (to) *exp.* to convince someone to do something.

usage example: Michelle said she didn't want to go with us to the movies. Why don't you try and **talk her into it**? I just know she'd have a good time.

translation: Michelle said she didn't want to go with us to the movies. Why don't you try to convince her? I just know she'd have a good time.

talk someone out of something (to) *exp.* to convince someone not to do something.

usage example: I was going to accept the job position of manager, but Earl **talked me out of it**. He said it would be too much work and long hours.

translation: I was going to accept the job position of manager, but Earl convinced me not to accept it. He said it would be too much work and long hours.

tee-tee (to go) *exp.* (baby talk) to urinate.

usage example: Do you have **to go tee-tee**?

translation: Do you have to go urinate?

tête-à-tête *exp.* (French) a private conversation between two people.

usage example: The boss is having a **tête-à-tête** with Richard. Do you think he's going to get fired?

translation: The boss is having a private conversation with Richard. Do you think he's going to get fired?

NOTE: This expression comes from French meaning a "head-to-head." In France, the pronunciation is *"tet-a-tet."*

However in America, it is commonly pronounced *"tate-a-tate."*

"That does it!" *exp.* "That's all I can tolerate!"

usage example: **That does it**! If you ever borrow anything from me again without asking, you're in big trouble!

translation: That's all I can tolerate! If you ever borrow anything from me again without asking, you're in big trouble!

SYNONYM: **"That tears it!"** *exp.*

usage example: **That tears it**! If the boss doesn't give me a raise, I'm quitting!

translation: That's all I can tolerate! If the boss doesn't give me a raise, I'm quitting!

"That's out of the question!" *exp.* "There is absolutely no way that will be considered!"

usage example: You want to borrow my car to haul fertilizer? That's **out of the question**!

translation: You want to borrow my car to haul fertilizer? There's absolutely no way I'd consider that!

"The early bird gets the worm" *exp.* "The person who begins his/her work the earliest gets all the opportunities and the most accomplished."

usage example: I like to get to work before anyone else. **The early bird gets the worm**.

translation: I like to get to work before anyone else. The person who begins his/her work the earliest gets the most accomplished.

VARIATION: **The early bird catches the worm** *exp.*

the last straw (to be) *exp.* to be all one can tolerate.

usage example: Our next door neighbors have been playing loud music since midnight. Now they're throwing empty bottles in our backyard! **That's the last straw**. I'm calling the police.

translation: Our next door neighbors have been playing loud music since midnight. Now they're throwing empty bottles in our backyard! That's all I'm going to tolerate. I'm calling the police.

VARIATION: **to be the straw that broke the camel's back** *exp.*

"The more the merrier" *exp.* "The more people involved in a particular activity, the more fun it will be."

usage example: Why don't you join us on our picnic today? **The more the merrier**!

translation: Why don't you join us on our picnic today? The more people involved, the more fun it will be!

"The shoe's on the other foot" *exp.* "The situation is reversed" (said when someone is forced to suffer the same situation that he/she has caused someone else to experience).

usage example: David's horrible old boss is now David's employee! Suddenly **the shoe is on the other foot**.

translation: David's horrible old boss is now David's employee! Suddenly the situation is reversed.

"There are plenty of other fish in the sea" *exp.* "There are many other opportunities in the world."

usage example: He's always so mean to you. Why don't you go find someone else? **There are plenty of other fish in the sea**.

translation: He's always so mean to you. Why don't you go find someone else? There are many other opportunities for you to meet someone.

"There's more than one way to skin a cat" *exp.* "There are many ways to achieve one's goal;" "There are lots of right ways to do something."

usage example: If you can't resolve your problem the first time, try another way. Remember, **there's more than one way to skin a cat**.

translation: If you can't resolve your problem the first time, try another way. Remember, there are many ways to achieve one's goal.

"There's no accounting for taste" *exp.* "There is no explanation for people's likes and dislikes.

usage example: Do you believe that Mike bought that horrible painting? One thing's for sure. **There's no accounting for taste**.

translation: Do you believe that Mike bought that horrible painting? One thing's for sure. There is no explanation for people's likes and dislikes.

through-and-through *exp.* in every respect, completely.

usage example: Kim's an actress **through-and-through**. She was in her first play at age five and still loves the theater.

translation: Kim's an actress in every respect. She was in her first play at age five and still loves the theater.

through a/the wringer (to put someone) *exp.* to put someone through a strenuous and emotional experience.

usage example: Why didn't you call to tell me you were going to be three hours late coming home? I was so worried. You really **put me through a wringer**!

translation: Why didn't you call to tell me you were going to be three hours late coming home? I was so worried. You really caused me a great deal of emotional turmoil!

NOTE: In the early days of washing machines, it was common to put the laundry through a device known as a *"wringer"* before hanging the clothing outside to dry. This device was comprised of two rollers between which the clothing was pressed, squeezing out any excess water. The above expression, depicts someone who is emotionally drained or *"squeezed"* dry.

tick-tock *exp.* the sound made by a clock (usually a pendulum clock).

usage example: The sound of my clock going **tick-tock** kept me awake all night.

translation: The sound of my clock ticking kept me awake all night.

tick-tocking *exp.*

usage example: Do you hear that **tick-tocking** coming from your neighbor's house?

translation: Do you hear that ticking sound coming from your neighbor's house?

tie the knot (to) *exp.* to get married.

usage example: Nancy and Dominic are going **to tie the knot** next week.

translation: Nancy and Dominic are going to get married next week.

SYNONYM: to get hitched *exp.* • (lit); to tie together.

usage example: I'm **getting hitched** tomorrow!

translation: I'm getting married tomorrow!

tip-top *exp.* the highest degree of excellence.

usage example: I feel **tip-top** today.

translation: I feel in the most excellent health today.

"To kill two birds with one stone" *exp.* "To accomplish two goals in one deed."

usage example: I have to take my sister to the airport by 2:00pm and pick up a friend at 3:00pm. This will be easy. I'll be able **to kill two birds with one stone**.

translation: I have to take my sister to the airport by 2:00pm and pick up a friend at 3:00pm. This will be easy. I'll be able to accomplish two goals at the same time.

"To make a long story short..." *exp.* "In summary..."

usage example: **To make a long story short**, Jeff is taking me to France next month!

translation: In summary, Jeff is taking me to France next month!

toe-to-toe (to go) *exp.* to debate or compete.

usage example: Joe and Ann **went toe to toe** on the issue of women's rights.

translation: Joe and Ann debated the issue of women's rights.

tom-tom *exp.* a small drum beaten with the hands.

usage example: My parents gave my little brother a set of **tom-toms** for his birthday. He plays them all day long!

translation: My parents gave my little brother a set of small drums for his birthday. He plays them all day long!

tum-tum *exp.* (baby talk) stomach.

usage example: You ate lots of ice cream today. Is your **tum-tum** full?

translation: You ate lots of ice cream today. Is your stomach full?

turn over a new leaf (to) *exp.* to change one's bad habits.

usage example: As usual, I overate and now I feel sick. Starting tomorrow, I'm **turning over a new leaf**.

translation: As usual, I overate and now I feel sick. Starting tomorrow, I'm giving up my bad habits.

two-by-two *exp.* one person next to the other.

usage example: I want you all to form a line **two-by-two**.

translation: I want you all to form a line one person next to the other.

SYNONYM: side-by-side *exp.*

U

unable to make heads or tails [out] of someone or something (to be) *exp.* to be unable to make sense of someone or something.

usage example: Sometimes Mark is so nice and other times he's so nasty. I just can't **make heads or tails [out] of** him.

translation: Sometimes Mark is so nice and other times he's so nasty. I just can't make sense of him.

up-and-up (to be on the) *exp.* to be candid and honest.

usage example: Do you think that politician is **on the up-and-up**?

translation: Do you think that politician is candid and honest?

V

vanish into thin air (to) *exp.* to disappear completely.

usage example: I was speaking with an elderly woman and turned away for just a few seconds. When I turned back, she had **vanished into thin air**!

translation: I was speaking with an elderly woman and turned away for just a few seconds. When I turned back, she had completely disappeared!

"Variety is the spice of life" *exp.* "People's differences make the world interesting."

usage example: My new roommate and I are so different. I hope we don't have any problems living together. I just have to remember that **variety is the spice of life**.

translation: My new roommate and I are so different. I hope we don't have any problems living together. I just have to remember that people's differences make the world interesting.

vim-and-vigor *exp.* energy, stamina.

usage example: Your mother went hiking with you? She must have lots of **vim-and-vigor**.

translation: Your mother went hiking with you? She must have lots of energy.

W

walk arm in arm (to) *exp.* to walk with one's arm curled through someone else's arm; arms linked or intertwined.

usage example: I think they're best friends. They always **walk arm in arm** everywhere they go.

translation: I think they're best friends. They always walk with their arms linked.

NOTE: SEE: *A CLOSER LOOK: More Repeating Words, p. 198*

waste someone (to) *exp.* to kill someone.

usage example: If you don't hand over your money right now, I'm gonna **waste** you!

translation: If you don't surrender your money right now, I'm going to kill you!

NOTE: *"Gonna"* is a common reduction for "going to."

"We'll cross that bridge when we come to it" *exp.* "We'll face that problem when it arises."

usage example: "I'm so nervous about my singing audition. What'll I do if they ask me to sing something I don't know?"
"You'll cross that bridge when you come to it."

translation: "I'm so nervous about my singing audition. What'll I do if they ask me to sing something I don't know?"
"You'll face that problem when it arises."

"We'll cross that bridge when we get to it" *exp.*

"We've got you covered" *exp.* "We're aiming our guns at you."

usage example: Surrender. **We've got you covered**!

translation: Surrender. We're aiming our guns at you.

NOTE: **to cover someone** *exp.* **1.** to aim a gun at someone • **2.** to protect someone by using a gun.

usage example: Surrender. **We've got you covered**!

translation: Surrender. We're aiming our guns at you!

NOTE: The difference between definitions **1.** and **2.** depends on the context.

"What gives?" *exp.* "What's happening?"

usage example: You all look so sad. **What gives**?

translation: You all look so sad. What's happening?

"When in Rome, do as the Romans [do]" *exp.* "One must adopt the habits of the local people."

usage example: I ate raw fish when I went to Japan. I figured "**when in Rome, do as the Romans [do]**."

translation: I ate raw fish when I went to Japan. I figured when you travel, practice the same customs as the natives.

VARIATION : This expression may simply be shortened to: **"When in Rome"** since the rest of the expression is merely inferred.

"When it rains, it pours" *exp.* "When an event occurs, it occurs with great intensity or frequency."

usage example: I got invited to ten parties tonight! **When it rains, it pours**!

translation: I got invited to ten parties tonight! When an event occurs, it occurs with great intensity!

VARIATION: **"It never rains, but it pours"** *exp.*

"When the cat's away, the mice will play" *exp.* "When the authorities are gone, mischief begins."

usage example: As soon as we left the house, our children invited their friends over for a wild party. **When the cat's away, the mice will play**.

translation: As soon as we left the house, our children invited their friends over for a wild party. When the authorities are gone, mischief begins.

"Where there's a will, there's a way" *exp.* "If something is desired enough, a means will be found to achieve it."

usage example: "How will I ever get enough money to go to Hawaii?" "**Where there's a will, there's a way**."

translation: "How will I ever get enough money to go to Hawaii?" "If you want it badly enough, you'll find a way."

Y

yick-yack *exp.* to talk or chatter meaninglessly.

usage example: Every time I see Jim, all he ever does is **yick-yack**!

translation: Every time I see Jim, all he ever does is talk and talk about nothing!

 VARIATION (1): **yickety-yack** *exp.*
VARIATION (2): **yackety-yack** *exp.*
VARIATION (3): **yack-yack** *exp.*

"You can't judge a book by its cover"
exp. "You can't judge something by how it looks on the outside."

usage example: I thought Beth was so nice at first. She looked so sweet and friendly. Then I discovered she's actually insensitive, mean, and jealous. One thing's for sure. **You can't judge a book by its cover.**

translation: I thought Beth was so nice at first. She looked so sweet and friendly. Then I discovered she's actually insensitive, mean, and jealous. One thing's for sure. You can't judge something by how it looks from the outside.

"You can't teach an old dog new tricks"
exp. "Old people can't learn new skills;"

"It's difficult to break an old pattern of behavior."

usage example: I'm seventy years old and I'm never going to be able to learn to use a computer. I'm afraid **you can't teach an old dog new tricks.**

translation: I'm seventy years old and I'm never going to be able to learn to use a computer. I'm afraid you can't teach old people new skills.

yum yum *exp.* used to indicate that something is delicious.

usage example: "Would you like a piece of chocolate cake?"
"**Yum yum**! I love chocolate cake!"

translation: "Would you like a piece of chocolate cake?"
"That sounds delicious! I love chocolate cake!"

ORDER FORM ON BACK

Prices subject to change

AMERICAN	BOOK	CASSETTE
STREET TALK -1	$16.95	$12.50
How to Speak and Understand American Slang		
STREET TALK -2	$16.95	$12.50
Slang Used in Popular American Television Shows		
STREET TALK -3	$18.95	$12.50
The Best of American Idioms		
BIZ TALK -1	$16.95	$12.50
American Business Slang & Jargon		
(general office • finance • meetings & negotiations • business travel • "computerese" • marketing & advertising)		
BIZ TALK -2	$16.95	$12.50
More American Business Slang & Jargon		
(international trade • hotel & tourism • hospitality • real estate • human resources • management • "bureaucratese" • legalese • politics)		
BLEEP!	$14.95	$12.50
A Guide to Popular American Obscenities		

FRENCH		
STREET FRENCH -1	$15.95	$12.50
The Best of French Slang		
STREET FRENCH -2	$15.95	$12.50
The Best of French Idioms (available September '96)		
STREET FRENCH -3	$15.95	$12.50
The Best of Naughty French (available September '96)		

SPANISH		
STREET SPANISH	$15.95	$12.50
How to Speak and Understand Spanish Slang		

GERMAN		
STREET GERMAN -1	$16.95	$12.50
The Best of German Idioms		

—— OPTIMA BOOKS Order Form ——

2820 Eighth Street · Berkeley, CA 94710

For U.S. and Canada, use our TOLL FREE FAX line: 1-800-515-8737
International orders FAX line: 510-848-8737 · Publisher direct: 510-848-8708

Name _____

(School/Company) _____

Street Address _____

City _____ State/Province _____ Postal Code _____

Country _____ Phone _____

Quantity	Title	Book or Cassette?	Price Each	Total Price

Total for Merchandise	
Sales Tax (California Residents Only)	
Shipping (See Below)	
ORDER TOTAL	

METHOD OF PAYMENT (check one)

☐ Check or Money Order   ☐ VISA   ☐ Master Card   ☐ American Express   ☐ Discover
(Money orders and personal checks must be in US funds and drawn on a US bank.)

Credit Card Number: **Card Expires:**

⬚⬚⬚⬚⬚⬚⬚⬚⬚⬚⬚⬚⬚⬚⬚⬚   ⬚⬚ ⬚⬚

Signature *(important!)*:

SHIPPING

Domestic Orders: SURFACE MAIL (delivery time 5-7 days).
Add $5 shipping/handling for the first item · $1 for each additional item.
RUSH SERVICE available at extra charge.

International Orders: OVERSEAS SURFACE (delivery time 6-8 weeks).
Add $6 shipping/handling for the first item · $2 for each additional item.
OVERSEAS AIRMAIL available at extra charge.

ST3